This book is dedicated
to all who feel they stand alone,
who sense there is no room in the inn
but who know that where they sit
to sup with Jesus they are Church
(after Luke 7: 49)

THE LAITY
HELP OR HINDRANCE?

A PASTORAL PLAN

JERRY JOYCE PP

MERCIER PRESS

Mercier Press
PO Box 5, 5 French Church Street, Cork
16 Hume Street, Dublin 2

© Jerry Joyce, 1994

A CIP record for this book is available from the British Library.

ISBN 1 85635 097 5

10   9   8   7   6   5   4   3   2   1

Cover design by Syd Bluett
Typeset by Richard Parfrey in Palatino 10/13
Printed in Ireland by ColourBooks Ltd. Baldoyle, Dublin 13

CONTENTS

FOREWORD

Faith in this parish of Clogh is strong. God has an important place in the people's lives. A spirit of love for each other is also evident. Suffering and hardships have been experienced here. But in such times of great need, love shines. Faith and love have been and are expressed in much diversity. This has not always happened in and through the Church as we knew it.

In the past a large section of this community's experience of the Church brought fear and doubt. They did not see themselves as acceptable or significant. Working-class people, mostly miners, were seen as uneducated, without views and opinions. They had no say in Church affairs. We had much love and respect for many of those miners. They shared with us all the best values of the gospel. Many were very spiritual, good-living, honest, kind and generous men. I know that the Holy spirit was alive and active in these men. When I think of 'being Church', their real Christian life makes the deepest impression on me.

This is remarkable because so many of them were regarded as communists. Each miner's family has a strong memory of the pain of that time. A number of those men who had been excommunicated by the Church did attract the attention of people who *were* communist – at a house meeting in Moneenroe a man called Brian O'Neill came to indoctrinate them. One of the miners thanked him for coming and for the benefit of the discussion. Mr O'Neill's reply is etched in the folklore memory of this community: 'That was no discussion,' he said. 'It was a duel of words; you are not communists but men merely seeking justice.' These excommunicated men never felt at home in their local Church again. However, their humour, wit and spirituality helped them to accept that God was on their side even if the people in the big houses and those with property believed them to be communists.

Perhaps this is why family life is still greatly valued in this community. There is a great sense of loyalty here. Each new-born child is welcomed with joy and seen as a gift from God. People care for each other. They give prominence to the love as shared in family life. I myself grew up in a family that instilled in me this view of life and faith. My father's 'keep in touch with God', taught me much more about faith and life as a journey than any religious teaching in school. However, his lack of trust in Church institutions, like that of many with his mining background, also stayed with me. Alongside that mistrust was a great reverence, respect, understanding and support for the priests doing their job in service to the parish. They were there when needed, for administering the sacraments, for prayer and devotions and as support in tragedy. But there was a link missing between what happened in our daily lives, our workplace, our community and what happened in Church.

While there was reverence and respect for the priest and his faithfulness to his duties, there was also a longing to break free: a desire to cry out that we too had received the gifts of the spirit; we too serve one another; we want not just to be a section of a community but to be the one Christian community. We want to be Church. This began to happen in the late 1960s. A young priest, Fr Frank Maher came to assist our then parish priest who was ailing. He had a different view of Church. It was like our own. Everyone felt involved. He talked of the changes brought by the Vatican Council. There was a buzz. There was energy and life. It was my first experience of 'a living expression of Eucharist in Community'. Sadly, he was transferred. Except for the few changes in the liturgy we were once again to stay put as Pre-Vatican II practice was reimposed.

1989 was a significant year for the parish. Two new priests were appointed. People can still recall little actions that symbolised for them that these men had time for our kind of Church. Amongst the most significant were their desire really to know, the quality of their listening and the almost immediate response in action that proved they heard what we were saying. Soon we were helping to make decisions. We saw a type of group energy emerging as we started doing things together. There was acceptance that things had not always been done right – that people had been hurt in the past by being excluded, even excommunicated.

Our new parish priest, Fr Jerry Joyce kept emphasising the community aspect of the parish: that communities need leaders and that these leaders come properly from within that community. He himself typified that leadership. Perhaps his leadership from within came from his willingness to admit to struggling, to searching, to suffering and to his own need of redemption. He knows human nature. He knows divine nature too. His God is like the Jesus in the gospel. Someone open to and in touch with people where they are on life's journey. He encouraged, supported, affirmed and challenged. We don't always agree with him nor he with us! But there is room for discussion. There is encouragement at achievement. There is joy in involvement. The Church is seen as good for community and helpful to our personal and spiritual growth.

Knowing what happened in the past when Fr Frank Maher left creates fear that the same will happen again. This is our concern now. A few of us had the help of a course in St Patrick's Seminary, Carlow to discuss that concern. The course, Parish Theory and Structure, was not just theory for us. It was a struggle to provide a way of making sure that the Church will continue to be a community in our parish; not just Catholic but happily Christian. The combined efforts of the Church of Ireland and our's work towards this unity.

This book delineates the role of the post-Vatican Council parish priest but it also highlights the responsibility of the laity in the modern Church. It is about a Church where individual care is combined with a pastoral plan to create a community of belonging and participation. It is about a community where Christ is the head and where Church structures are evolving instruments responsive to the guidance of the spirit.

It is about what happens at the grassroots – the most voiceless yet most living organ of the body of Christ. It is about the people's model of Church where love and sharing are the pillars of our faith.

The family is our model of Church. It is the small community that reflects the relationship between God and his people. In this International Year of the Family we are at last beginning to believe that the family is of primary importance and value in the vision that the Church has of its own life. The invitation to discern God's will for our families and for the family of the parish has brought a new meaning to prayer. It took a change of practice to convince us that the Church believes that Christ does not merely come with the priest but that he is already in our home, in the love that is the living-out of our vocation. Where love is we know that God is there too. Where two or three gather in his name Christ is present.

We always got the impression that the authorities had a keen interest in large crowds in Church. The real love, faith and hope in the family got little practical attention. All the official energy went into what happened in the Church; very little energy went into helping homes to be places of happiness and spiritual growth. With the exception of baptism, first holy communion and confirmation, when are we ever helped to be 'Church'? It seems that the home has always to come to the Church to be regarded as Church! A fear of communism made the clergy reject our families' Christian, painful, struggle for justice. Clergy and people were both victims of the culture of the day – fear of communism and the acceptance of poor living conditions for the miners by those who were property owners. Sometimes to tolerate the culture is to become prisoners of society.

Modern culture is having the same effect upon the aspirations of our youth to a new way today. We have positive plans that are good for community. Few outside this community want to hear about them. From criticisms in the papers we discovered how easy it is to be misrepresented. Even when we tried to respond to misrepresentation the national media denied us the right to reply. Thankfully the local media continue to be attentive to the differing voices within community. They reflect the riches of diversity.

Does history repeat itself? Are we always to be victims of the international and national culture as reflected by the media? At present we feel the consolation that the Church has joined us where we have been for sixty years. A positive vision of life is something for which we hunger. Our parish priest's talent is to allow human life as it is lived by us ordinary people to express this vision. It was most difficult to get him to put it in book form. Yet if it is on the record in the context of the things we all do together there is a better chance that the vision will survive. This book is that record. For us it is like good news that you want to share. Though we had many good reasons why this book should be written Fr Jerry did not share our enthusiasm! However, his participation in the summer of 1992 in a conference in Nova Scotia changed his view. Delegates from priests' councils from all the English-language countries in the world met to plan renewal according to the mind of Vatican II. Convinced that we were on the right road, that others needed to know that the Church sought by the Vatican Council is good, he agreed to put it in writing.

After reading what he has written here I hope that you too will agree that what the people desire in their hearts and in their lives is good for the Church. What the book does not solve is our fear and concern about lack of continuity. It is twenty-five years since Fr Frank Maher came to us with his Vatican Council vision. It took the appointment of a classmate of his as parish priest to restore that vision. Is there a way of keeping it, irrespective of who the leader is? Concrete pastoral action in every English speaking parish in the world must feel the pain of that anxiety. We now know that our views and opinions are worthy of consideration. Somehow, they must become a major element in the pastoral priorities of the Church. Then the reforms of the Vatican Council will become a reality. Praying for that continuity I invite your response to what you are about to read.

Mai Dormer

PROLOGUE

In 1957 Pius XII spoke of a new springtime in the Church. There was a buzz of excitement with the appointment of John XXIII in 1958. In Church Unity week in 1959 he announced Vatican II.[1] What an exhilarating time to begin studying for the priesthood? We all saw signs of providence when a torrential down-pour turned to sunshine on 11 October 1962 as John XXIII opened the Council in the presence of thousands of bishops (perfectly happy with a monarchical and hierarchical Church!)

John XXIII began a revolution. Declaring a new Pentecost he invited the council fathers to 'interpret the signs of the times'. This was a unique departure from the traditional system of looking at principles and drawing conclusions. Now they were focusing on the world. The prophets were called to assist in touching the lived reality. These experts known as *periti* brought with them the fruits of the biblical, liturgical, ecumenical and catechetical movements that had already been given great freedom by Pope Pius XII.

More scriptural images for Church replaced the 'perfect society' model then in use. This resulted in a radical, dynamic constitution for the Church itself – the first ever? This was after Cardinal Suenens and Cardinal Montini (later Paul VI) had the Curia's document on the nature of the Church juridical and militant rejected for a 'people of God' approach. The attitude of the Church in the world was changed. Liturgy as the 'face of the Church in the world' was revolutionised. Scripture took over from formulae and norms as the heart and inspiration of all the council's 'fruits'. And the rest is history...

Or is it? Are we drifting back towards the dogmatism, clericalism, legalism and triumphalism banished by the council? Have the words collegiality, community, service and pastor been replaced again by judicial rites with power re-invested at the top of a hierarchical model of Church? Do synods and pastoral councils really have a collaborative methodology of participation, with co-responsibility at all levels? A 'message to the people of God' from the Extraordinary Synods of Bishops in 1985 keeps the dream alive.

At its AGM in September 1986 the National Conference of Priests of Ireland urged our bishops to produce a national pastoral plan.[2] The NCPI viewed 'with admiration' parishes where the laity, religious and clergy are involved together in the task of building Christian community. The elected re-presentatives of the priests of Ireland went on to express their belief that 'this partnership is vital to the success of the apostolate of Ireland'.

They recommended 'that a way be devised to ensure that lay people have a voice in producing this pastoral plan at national and diocesan level'. They advocated 'the full involve-ment of women in decision-making in the Church'. They stressed the 'urgent need for priests to be prepared for a new kind of leadership role among their people'. They requested that 'individual bishops support the production of a diocesan pastoral plan to develop partnership in ministry between people and priests'.

This call for partnership by the priests of Ireland at the AGMs from 1985 onwards has taken longer than expected to become a reality. Structures for partnership must be con-structed from the bottom up where real relationships occur. Principles emerging from experience provide authentic structures. Otherwise we reinforce the monarchical hierarchical Church model.

Here in this parish of Clogh we have set out to implement this specific call of the NCPI in response to the 1987 synod on the laity and the call by John Paul II for renewal of the Church. As the NCPI said in 1985 'many people are searching out what it means to be active members of the Church'. But with our tradition of authoritarianism and the consequent subservience in people, they need an initial leadership. That leadership is provided with the following six principles as a framework:

(i)   That union with God in Christ Jesus through the Spirit is the communion/participation at the heart of being Church.

(ii)   That the Vatican II and synodal documents already provide enough ideas, principles and guidelines for a real pastoral renewal.

(iii) That renewed structures need a renewed people and vice versa, if the spirit of that council is to permeate the parish and society.

(iv)   The most effective leadership process is collaboration. Its primary goal is to identify, release, utilise and unify the gifts of all baptised Christians. This involves an explicit, continuous, deliberate chosen and sustained effort prayerfully to share discernment, decision-making and evaluation at every level.

(v)   That without the presence of the spirit and conformity to the will of Christ we labour in vain.

(vi)   That the council brought a profound change in the role of the priest.

The Council of Trent had concentrated on priestly *power*, especially to consecrate the bread and wine and to forgive sins and to share in the office and dignity of the bishop.[3] In practice the ethos of conferring an office rather than the sacrament of orders set the priorities. A system of canonical appointment, with everything under the jurisdiction of the local bishop, whose power was absolute, was the outcome. Subservient obedience was the norm.

Vatican II brought a new emphasis: service is the essence of priesthood. It is shared with the bishop. It is Christ however who acts in the sacraments. So it is Christ rather than the bishop whom the priest is now seen to represent. The call to priesthood, like the call to utilise the gifts and charisms of all the baptised comes from God. The priesthood shares in the priesthood of Christ primarily as teacher, then as sanctifier and finally as leader. There is not much time for administration or for training the local team or for dropping around regularly to all the houses!

All ministry is a direct response to the gifts God has bestowed – and they are a variety of gifts to be used. Collaborative ministry, bringing together all the various gifts to accomplish the mission of Jesus, still has a few surprises in store. Universally, with the exception of a change to the local language in liturgy and a few new committees, all the work of the council has yet to begin.

This book is dedicated to those who believe that the council 'ain't over until it's over'. Archbishop Hayes of Halifax rejuvenated our vision with that pungent phrase when he animated a meeting in Nova Scotia of delegates from priests councils in sixteen English-speaking countries in August 1992.

It is particularly dedicated to people like Dr Birch, my first bishop, who was a council father. He pushed many of us past subtle elements of resistance, (motivated by inadequacy and failure perhaps) towards actually channelling energy, time, prayer and money into trying to make some little bit of it a reality.

Colleagues in youth service, in community radio, in ecumenical action, in secular educational institutions at Leicester and Swansea, and a variety of laity groups have been profoundly influential. The parish team at Clogh, Castlecomer, Co. Kilkenny where I am now PP have been most influential in drawing it all together in the service of one community. The affirmation provided by the work itself, the dedicated service of so many parishioners and the enriching spiritual friendship of so many in religious life have empowered me in my weakest moments.

There are many people who, through retreats, national and international conferences, seminars, lectures have stimulated my ideas, reflections and actions. They may recognise some of their own experience in these pages! Some have been profoundly influential in stimulating the application of the gospel to my personal and pastoral lives.

I am especially grateful for the faith, wisdom and love of the families in whose parishes I have served as a priest. There are many apostles and prophets. They were the unseen strength in my growth to a deeper understanding of our human and Christian life. Parents, family and friends, nurtured the child within – calling me out from hiding.

This book is not a consequence of study, research or reading. It is a product of experience. I wish to thank all who have touched my life and illuminated the experience. May God bless them all.

---

1   The word 'council' refers to the teaching of Vatican II whenever it is used in this book.
2   Quotations are taken from a file of reports and summaries from meetings of the NCPI in my personal possession.
3   The Council of Trent took place between 1545 and 1563. It was the nineteenth ecumenical council of the church and tackled many of the abuses that had motivated the Protestant Reformation. It issued many doctrinal decrees including the definition of the mass as a true sacrifice. Its decrees were issued in a summary statement by Pius IV in 1564.

CHAPTER 1

EVOLUTIONARY CHANGE

RESPECTING THE LIVING

Life is a story. There are countless stories, more than there are lives. Every sentence of what is written here has come from someone's story. It is in the living experience that the life of God flows. The Bible, the world, the schoolbook, the community, the people are the media of a million real stories. God's love is there somewhere in them all.

Our stories are becoming more and more public. The pains and the traumas in the relationships of the significant people form the main preoccupation of much of modern culture. Sometimes the sensation in the story unbalances the grandeur of the total picture. We are invited to view the person through the brokenness and the wounds. We are shocked. We are in pain. Sometimes we are scandalised by the sight.

We often forget that this was the image of Calvary seen by Mary and the disciples of Jesus. Calvary was an unpleasant sight. Paul called it a scandal for the religious ones (the Jews) and a folly for the pagan ones (the Gentiles). Yet because of that one story all other stories have a profoundly different meaning. Seeing life through the wounded is looking at it through the heart of our God. His unconditional love never makes anyone feel a disgrace.

Our perspective on the gospel and our view of this great and good person who is wounded out of love for us is not always accurate. We see him as remote or distant, seldom as the companion for the road, particularly when we are dejected or downcast (cf. Luke 24). Even when we need healing and help we are not convinced that Jesus is the way.

It was on the First Friday that I visited Jack and Mary. Jack was blind. He was unwell when I visited. I decided to anoint him. He agreed. I read the gospel story of Jesus curing the blind man. That afternoon his wife Sheila (who was always shopping when I visited) called to see me. When I opened the door, without any greeting she immediately cried, 'You were out with Jack today!' She paused for breath. I waited. Then she said, 'You told him a story of a man who was blind and got cured. Who cured him?'

'Jesus,' I replied. Never have I seen a person turn immediately and walk away with such disappointment on her face!

I recalled another incident of that same morning. On my previous visit to Mary I was caught for time and omitted the reading of scripture. Instead I said some pious aspirations. When I began to read the scripture that morning, the ninety-two year old lifted her head and shouted, 'Stop.' I waited. She said, 'I would rather if you gave me a holier communion like you did last month.'

When all is said and done it is we ourselves, all of us individually, who have to connect our personal story with the story of Jesus. Our own openness of heart and our desire to meet Jesus – not as a thing, or in a thing or magical ritual, but as a person – is the key to that connection.

When we look at the story in the lives of all those touched by Jesus, everywhere we see aspects of our own story. No matter what we do for parish or community however splendid the organisation or the ritual, if the real story is absent, the exercise is in large part futile.

The old woman who got up and dragged in the turf and sticks during the day surprised her son when he called to do it as usual in the evening. He asked her why she hadn't waited. She replied: 'I'm tired of the things you do for me; sit and talk to me ...' I was reminded of Pope John Paul II's call to all engaged in the work of the Lord – not to forget the Lord of the work.

Statia and her daughter – both old-age pensioners – lived together. My greeting as I entered the house came from the culture of my childhood. They were the first words to be said by the disciples on entering a house according to Jesus' instruction. When I would say, 'Peace be to this house', the two women would respond with a hearty laugh. They never stopped 'chewing the rag', but it was a language of love. The daughter died soon after the mother, her absence making a desert, devoid of the water of love. The meaning of the contact and its depth far surpasses the ritual of action or word.

Then there was John, whom the priest visited at Christmas and Easter. 'That is the way he wanted it' they said. When I called, his eyes were full of fear and anxiety. His voice sounded agitated and he appeared to be unwelcoming. Yet his response to that same salutation was warm and came from a lifetime of repetition. It dissolved the icicles. Our chat grew friendly. I told him that I was about to give him absolution for *all* the sins of his lifetime. 'All of them, Father?' 'All of them,' I replied. This was repeated three times and when I added, 'All the sins you didn't tell, couldn't tell or forgot to tell,' the tension left his eyes. They filled up with tears. He relaxed a little into the chair and said, almost in a sigh from his heart, 'Sure you couldn't tell them all in the auld days, Father – sure they would ate the face of ya.' From then on communion might be brought to him everyday if it were possible. John's purgatory was over. He *knew* God is merciful and heals our shame.

The most touching part of being a priest is the daily un-known contact with 'God's own people'. Knowing the personal story of so many courageous individuals makes us walk humbly with our God. Each day there are special times where struggles are shared in private and confidentially. Such moments take us to the very heart of pastoral concern. In prayer too this is our first priority. The faith, love and hope of so many splendid Christians is a true witness to the Spirit's presence. In family life such daily witness brings mission alive in our community. Those witnesses are often the hidden but indispensable media of the body of Christ, daily perpetuating his redemptive action into our time and place. In the end what matters is the love and the communion it brings in, with and through Christ with the Father. Many a pre-Vatican priest is numbered amongst those witnesses.

Today there is a need to listen to each person's story so that our witness can give us authenticity in a changing society.

II
IN A CHANGING SOCIETY

Pastoral care is primarily for and about ordinary people. Pastoral wisdom comes from the experience of being a Christian and a priest in a changing Ireland. A modern Catholic perspective welcomes change, accepting it as inevitable and ongoing. It is also an essential aspect of our response to an invitation written in our hearts by God (cf. Isa. 54). As persons and communities we must change and grow.

God invites us to grow in body, mind, and spirit. After adolescence the body's growth is renewal – a total change in seven years! In perception, wisdom and understanding, the development of the spirit knows no limits of time or space. Its expansion is like the rings in the big oak tree – from within – rather than the rungs of an expanding ladder.

The stages of moral growth should now be familiar to most of the population. Each household is in touch with them through the reformed primary school religion programme. In its introduction, Kohlberg's three stages are summarised, from the pre-moral level through conformist morality, to self-accepted moral principles.[1] We retain an element of each of these stages throughout our lives. In terms of our motives for morality they rise from fear of punishment and hope of reward through desire for social approval or respect for law and order, to respect for the rights of people and appreciation of the general principles of goodness and justice. Much of the ethos of our pre-Vatican II Church put the emphasis on fear and reward as motives for morality. All parents are now aware that this is appropriate for the child only at the early stage.

James Fowler (*Stages of Faith*) has also charted for us the stages of religious growth.[2] His third stage is the one where the language of life changes. This was the point where the faith journey of many pre-Vatican II Catholics ended. At that stage there is a deep desire for belonging but without active commitment, passionate loyalty but avoidance of personal decision, a strong group identity but individually largely inarticulate, solidarity in behaviour and dress but with little emotional or mystical adventure. The result is an unreflective faith with a great feeling of belonging but unease with complexity. These are the characteristics of adolescence. Are they not also the hallmark of much fundamentalism?

After each stage there is a period of unease with what has come before which awakens us to our next phase. Passively belonging is not adequate for a complex adult society. Our Vatican II style Church and the social situation of modern Ireland now challenge us to move to a more mature adult phase. We are looking for a faith rooted in personal decision. We search for choice. We are critically alert. There is a kind of crisis that distances us from the conventional. In today's Ireland there is much that is similar to the characteristics of the life of the maturing adult.

How many adults distanced from the conventional are not aware that their crisis is a crucial phase of their human and faith development? They need reassurance that they have not 'lost the faith'. It is at parish level we discover that the modern Irish Church is a Church for the adult – a place of choice, personal decision and commitment.

The collapse of clarity may be distressing too for parents whose beliefs remain at the adolescent stage of their faith journey, one that is characterised by blind obedience. Their critical, alert and apparently unbelieving young adult children cause them great disappointment and pain. In the old world of faith, three out of six stages of growth were adequate for them. It is not giving sufficient nourishment now for their adult children. Because of the children's challenge the parents too reach a crisis. Our parish strives to introduce such parents to an adult Church, capable of helping them to understand the faith development of the modern young adult. In the complex social environment of our secularised modern Ireland, we inevitably move to choice and freedom from our authoritarian control in family, religious and social life.

The critically alert believer is invited to look at the Church as it is today. Those who are unhappy with aspects of the Church as they experience it are invited to discover that a Church of control is not the modern model. In fact at parish level such a Church is disappearing. Partnership in participation and decision-making is now the norm.

Those who are alienated now have a real opportunity to become agents of change rather than its victims. Their situation is a prophetic opportunity for the Irish people to bring a new spiritual richness to a united Europe which has long awaited this phase of religious development. We can be leaders in helping emerging Eastern European countries in particular to move from subservience to free choice, from the conventional to the decision-making phase of faith development.

We urge commentators who write in anger, out of their experience of hurt, to move on from interpreting and presenting Catholicism as if it hadn't changed since the 1950s. Their innate sense of justice must recognise that there is a diversity of ways to Jesus, even in modern Catholicism. The secular media, even in Ireland, present a dark and negative view of Catholicism, undervaluing its contribution to civic growth and development. This contribution being made through the commitment of Irish Catholics is considerable. Our own approach in this community and the ecumenical, Christian, human, person-centred values from which we operate contribute to a human enrichment which has been misrepresented. The comment and interpretation put on it by some tabloids is cynical in the extreme. Such cynicism is a disease that has to be identified and treated. It can be destructive of the bonding elements in society as a whole.

We tell it as we see it, in the context in which we live it and as we come to understand it. Recent shocks do not disturb us. We work in mutual acceptance of vulnerability and weakness. Our Church is one where we are all sinners, being redeemed by the only saviour, Jesus. We all have an equality of dignity with different rather than superior roles, with only one Lord, one teacher, one father, and he is merciful and just.

This rich variety gives new hope in the renewal process and encouragement in the face of a cynical secularism. A new spirit of dialogue initiated with commitment and dedication by priests at parish level had brought a whole new way of serving humanity in today's Ireland.

III
THROUGH A SPIRIT OF DIALOGUE

The bishops of Ireland addressed a special message to priests, religious, teachers, catechists, parents and youth leaders during International Youth Year in 1985. Their message was an invitation to a new dialogue with the whole people of God. For many of us this 1985 pastoral brought new hope. It was one of the few Irish episcopal documents that could not have been written if Vatican II had not happened.

It was encouragingly different from the vision of Church contained in the Code of Canon Law published in 1983. The bishops acknowledged that the way young people look at life, 'invites us to widen our religious horizons so as to include all the wounded world and to respond to it like Christ.' The young have little patience 'with narrow views, or anything that seems lacking in humanity'. The bishops were taking up the call of Pope John Paul II for a change of approach – a necessity if we are to make contact with the new generation, 'which is like a tinent to be won for Christ'.

This letter to the Young Church, with its direct appeal to young people heralded a new openness. It listed the characteristics of the modern Irish Church.[3]

- To all, including those 'who feel hostile to the Church', a time of *listening* was promised, 'to appreciate your hurts, your angers, your hopes, your attitudes in many areas including your experience in the Church in Ireland now'.

- The image of the Church favoured is 'the community of the friends of Jesus, those who follow his way, those who are guided by his spirit'. It is the 'place where he can be encountered in a rich variety of ways'. There was praise for those renewing the image and for the many excellent initiatives, 'that have tried *in imaginative ways to find the appropriate language for faith today*'.

- The importance of the 'authority of experience' was acknowledged for the first time. 'What carries most weight with young people is not what they are told by "authority". What they believe is what they experience for themselves.' With this emphasis on experience were noted other 'vital marks of the young generation', a search for friendship and a sensitivity to issues of justice. Youth's dissatisfaction 'with an impersonal society, or with a Church that does not seem to offer a genuine community' was acknowledged. As a consequence, the bishops went on to offer the young people '*a Church of community and participation*, as *the* way of faith in the future'.

- The bishops radically recognised 'this most purifying moment in our history, inviting all generations to a new level and language of faith – *less complacent, less preoccupied with the institution, less in control of every situation*. Out of this moment of challenge a renewed community of believers must come to birth – patiently, but not too slowly. *If it were too cautious, it might fail the fields ripe for the harvest now.*'

- Among the other 'rich elements of our Catholic tradition' the bishops spelled out 'six graced roads to discovering

Jesus as Lord'. The *solidarity* of belonging to a welcoming Church, the *service* of others, the *sacraments*, the *Sunday mass*, *scripture*, and *silence* (creating a space for prayer and for allowing the word of God to change us). 'At no time in the history of Irish Catholicism, has there been such marvellous diversity of groups, involving people of all ages, in the deepening of their faith and in the service of others.'

- The task of the Church is equated with the challenge of our time – the struggle to give time to humanity and to Christ. The bishops went on to say that 'Our wounded world cries out in so many ways; our dreams and our fears wrestle with one another. Left to one's self, each of us can be tempted to withdraw from the crucial struggle. It is Jesus who calls us into community as friends and then gives us power to give hope to the world.' Those who see the Church as a business of bishops and priests identified with its merely institutional aspects, are challenged by the bishops' call for 'the kind of Church that can meet the search for community, make sense of life and our desire to find and follow Christ in this world now, and the hunger to live generous lives that will bring hope to others.'

  This kind of Church 'will depend greatly on the imaginative communication of faith, through the Church at local level, through the renewal of catechetics in school, through the daily witness of parents and the support of believing families.'

- There is a need for a change in our image of God also. For some it is superstitious, 'the image of the punishing puppet-master, who has to be humoured and pacified in case he might pull the wrong string'. Others picture him as a distant inaccessible authority figure, who is totally out of tune with the compassionate friend held out to us in Christ. A surprising number of people look on God as a kind of clockmaker, a God of explanation for the universe, but irrelevant to ordinary life. For many more he is the God of the gaps, with no compelling existence until favours are needed or trouble strikes. But the only God worth believing in is the God who believed enough in people to die for us. The only God worth living for is the one who calls us to live in him, through dark faith in this life and in face to face fullness beyond death. *The only God worth searching for is the one who searches for us, and who still struggles within us, in order that we may become more free to love.'*

- This vision of Church with it pastoral priorities and initiatives, inspires us to create a community Church of participation, guided more by the authority of experience than the regulations of the institution. The bishops believe that 'there are many more on the periphery of the Church's life who would be equally committed if only they were motivated and involved'.

In our parish we believe Christ's assurance that the coming of his Spirit would be an infusion of Power (Acts 1: 8). We try to be open to that spirit that helps us see that we cannot minister on our own. We grow and change and live our ministry with an openness to changing together, freeing ourselves of the roles and closed titles that are an obstacle to collaboration.

IV
GROWING TOGETHER

We often invoke the Holy Spirit. We know that it is he who 'renews the face of the earth'. To do so he 'fills the heart of the faithful and enkindles in us the fire of his love'. It is by such love we change. Change may not always be good or welcome but it is inevitable today. Our personal renewal and pastoral performance is largely ineffective if it does not contain processes for coping with this fact. We, like our people, acquire attitudes, values, priorities and morals from family, peer groups, media influence and our social context. The structures of traditional Catholicism therefore, as well as our personal lives, need urgent and constant renewal. Vatican II accepted, before the majority of our parishioners were born, that our world had moved from a 'static concept of reality to a dynamic and evolutionary one.'[4] 'Traditional institutions, laws and modes of thought and emotion do not always appear to be in harmony with today's world. There is a completely new atmosphere that conditions the practice of religion.'

Our journey into discipleship is done in and through Christ's 'community of believers'. We are members of his Church as God's family in a time and place, where relationships are lived in rapidly and constantly changing circumstances. It is in this local family of God that we are drawn from unbelief to discipleship, from self-centredness to self-giving towards unconditional love.

In the family, who is perfect? Yet, love and loyalty enables acceptance of the struggles, faults, failings and sins of all its members. There is forgiveness for the wrongdoer, healing for the wounded, protection for the weak. Nobody is expected to be perfect. Wholeness is an ideal. Love strives to be *unconditional*, like God's love. There is a sense of core values that will be permanent in the human and spiritual journey even if imperfectly lived. Is it not primarily by the witness of his own life needing change and growth, that this sinful servant, the priest, leads the development of community in the spirit of a family whose head, Jesus, loves *unconditionally*? Does he not share the same journey as his people who are a community rooted and founded on love? This liberation from pretence assists in accepting that a Church of control is inappropriate, both to the world in which we live and to the gospel of Jesus. In such communities, families can still be the core of society in a time of dynamic and evolutionary change. Will such liberation not free the priest of 'closed' titles and roles and enable him to be a collaborating brother – a leader in responding to the fundamental command of Jesus? Even if we fail since we 'have love for one another', then all will know that we are his disciples. Our life must welcome 'the saving and healing power of Christ. We have no other saviour.'[5]

God is love. True human love is a divine power drawing out the humanity in us. It is responsive to our condition, needs, hungers, weaknesses, hurts and anxieties. It knows our contradictions, absurdities, miseries, envies, meanness, alienations, isolations and our self-centred irresponsibility. What it conveys is sympathy, understanding, compassion, acceptance and hence healing and growth.

Real love allows us to be what we are, to dare to be ourselves. There is no fear of rejection, condemnation or rebuke. It accepts. It understands. It asks us to put on nothing but to be what we are. It does not expect us to be better or worse. It just expects us to be.

It is our caring friends who give birth to and continue to nourish a sense of self which enables us to accept the self that we are. They enable us to laugh at and enjoy the real self. They continue to help us to feel our own insecurity, weakness and shame, but in a way which helps us to see them in the broader context of intentions, struggles, hopes, achievements and our overall commitment to them, to other people and to God.

We continue to grow only if we are enabled to identify and accept our feelings of hurt, fear, anger, resentment, alienation and guilt. This helps us to recognise which 'problems' are really ours, and which are those of the people, with whom we need to relate rather than desire to change.

Communication experts insist that our non-verbal communication and the way we go about it says far more than the verbal or intellectual content. We all need to know who we really are, what we are really saying by our life. What are our most hidden motives in all that we say and do? Inadequate self-knowledge can cause untold damage to the credibility of our 'declared' intentions. A spirituality of vulnerability permits us to recognise our weaknesses as well as our strengths. It assists us in acquiring real self-knowledge while still loving ourselves.

If 'authority' associates the affective aspects of our personality with our weak, corrupt and sinful part only, this self-knowledge is not possible. Persons with feelings, imagination, awareness and creativity will inevitably be 'knocked' rather than affirmed. Many people involved less with thoughts than with feelings or those who think about feelings are not encouraged to express their questioning or searching instincts. Does this seriously block out the voice of the Spirit? Life is more than logic and the intellectually high sounding 'well-ordered' arrangement of reality. This doubtful ideal sometimes seems to be regarded by Church rules as the sign of the presence of grace, beauty and truth.[6]

The salvation of the individual comes through conversion. Love is the *source and summit* of the Church's life and its supreme value. However, the Church and society through norms, roles, expectations, rules and structures considerably modifies a convert's self-expression. We are trying to change this. Our authority must not stifle the Spirit. People willing to be converted anew are formed and encouraged to love through the Church in word and deed. We are all merely pilgrims – broken and in need of healing. But we are not alone. We recognise as priests that to be truly in communication exposes our limitations and sinfulness.

V

AS COMMUNICATING SINNER

'The honest and humble acceptance of our frailty liberates us from pretence, from the effort of seeking to impress others and to justify ourselves.' Cardinal Hume in his book, *To be a Pilgrim*, goes on to say, 'in this way we can welcome into our lives the saving and healing power of Christ. We have no other saviour.' He points out, that one of the few prayers we can pray with total sincerity is, 'God be merciful to me a sinner.'[7]

Priests often feel the burden of their own sinfulness. Yet people treat us as the 'bread of God' or even the 'baker', rather than the 'beggars' who can tell other hungry ones where to find the bread. Thankfully as bread that is broken, we do become

Bread of Life.

Our availability presupposes vulnerability, a willingness to be broken. Acceptance of weakness and powerlessness makes room for the power of the Spirit. In working to build a world according to the heart of Jesus – to help people grow, to create, make or do, to improve the social and cultural environment in an intimate and human way – exposes our limitations and sinfulness. We know we need help. Choosing the road of involvement, working with rather than for people is both a pastoral plan and a risking of our humanity. When we are truly in communication people know our limitations and our sinfulness.

To be truly human is to be primarily in a state of communication and relationship. Only thus do we become effective communicators of the Word. Through Vatican II preaching the gospel was restored as the central mission of the priest.[8] As builders of the kingdom, we discovered that communication is about perception and understanding rather than mere words spoken. Communication is more about attitude and action than word, ritual or rule and is the soul of relationship.

Developing a Christian vision of the world in relationship with others, the environment and God, can occur only in the complexity of our daily struggles. The capacity to see God's presence both in the important events of life and in the ordinary activities of people grows out of lived experience and reflection. Living the faith is the real content of faith. Irish spirituality is characterised by a strong awareness of God's presence in creature and creator. The mystery of the unity and trinity of God is relationship. We name that relationship truth, love, spirit. It is in the power of that relationship that Christians are enabled in mind, heart, and spirit to see 'the mystery, the grandeur, and the beauty of human love touched by the divine'.[9]

The Irish bishops assert that 'to be deprived of love is a form of malnutrition'. The circle of love which unites parents with one another and their children is as necessary for the stability of children's personalities as food and clothing are for their bodily health. A lack of love makes it difficult to form a relationship with a God who is love'.[10]

We view our parish as family. We see its mission accomplished by the creation of a circle of love. It is the soil where the seed planted by the Spirit develops into relationships that are growth-promoting and enriching. Families rich in love reflect the beauty of life in the Spirit. Such families and parishes identify and cope with the forces, pressures, allurements and deceptions that masquerade as providers of the good life but are in fact only harbingers of disillusionment and the degradation of human dignity.

'I love you' is perhaps the most spoken phrase of modern history. However, it has a great diversity of meaning. To hear these words is for some affirming and encouraging. They express openness to expectations, wishes, joys, pains, hopes, thoughts and dreams. They invite the sharing of feelings, where warmth, affection and love in acceptance and trust encourage non-possessive and non-restrictive behaviour. Was that how the young people at Galway in 1979 for the papal visit heard it from Pope John Paul II?

For others the words 'I love you' are so expressed as to contain a threat, with the opposite effects. They demand a rigidity of roles and norms which stifle growth. This distortion results in friction, dispute, competitiveness, jealousy, rivalry, blame and possessiveness. The result is a closed style of relationship. This is often characterised by imposed decisions. The outcome is withdrawal or apathy, indifference or anger, accompanied by a suppression of feelings, arguments and judgmental remarks. Is that how those who are angry at the institutional Church hear it?

The human, pastoral and spiritual journey is a voyage of discovery into the diversity of the meaning of love. We priests too are unveiled as sinful servants. Many traditional Catholic values and the institutional role expectations of the priest are both a hindrance and a help in our acceptance of the love of

Jesus. His is open rather than closed love. The Bible is primarily the story of unconditional love. 'The saints in every age agree, "Love is all". It is enough to love. Our judgment will be totally concerned on whether we have loved and how we have loved.'[11]

In a rapidly fragmenting society, the external break-up will only be healed by accepting this inner reality of unconditional love. 'And so it becomes all the more urgent to steep ourselves in the truth that comes from Christ, who is "the way, the truth and the life" (John14: 6), and in the strength the he himself offers through his Spirit.' Pope John Paul II reminded us of this in his Phoenix Park homily (29 Sept 1979).[12] He was advising us on how to cope with a 'new kind of confrontation, with values and trends that until now had been alien to Irish society'. If only our weak fragile love had that enriching touch of the divine spark!

---

1   Lawrence Kohlberg, an American development research psychologist was influenced by the work of an earlier twentieth century expert Jean Piaget on the relationship between 'nature and nurture'. He has many insights as to how we unite our evolutionary history with our particular experiences in the world. There are many observable qualitative changes in each person's moral reasoning. Differences in reasoning may give different meaning to identical responses evoked at various developmental stages. Kohlberg classifies three stages of moral reasoning. The first stage, in decisions about right and wrong a child judges by the external causes of pain and pleasure. In the second stage the child acts as others expect. By the third stage we have learned that rules and institutions are not absolute – phase most difficult to reach in an authoritarian social milieu. (*Religious Programme Book for Primary Schools*)

2   J. W. Fowler, *Stages of Faith: A Brief Summary*:
Primal faith: (Infancy): A pre-language disposition of trust forms in the mutuality on one's relationships with parents and others to offset the anxiety that results from separations which occur during infant development.
Intuitive-projective faith: (Early childhood): Imagination, stimulated by stories, gestures, symbols and not yet controlled by logical thinking, combines with perception and feelings to create long-lasting images that represent both the protective and threatening powers surrounding one's life.
Mythic-literal faith: (Childhood and beyond): The developing ability to think logically helps one order the world categories of causality, space and time, to enter into the perspectives of others and to capture life

meaning in stories.

Synthetic-conventional faith: (Adolescence and beyond): New cognitive abilities make mutual perspectives-taking possible and requires one to integrate diverse self-images into a coherent identity. A personal and largely unreflective synthesis of beliefs and values evolves to support identity and to unite one in emotional solidarity with others.

Individuative-reflective faith (Young adulthood and beyond): Critical reflection upon one's beliefs and values, utilising third-person perspective taking; understanding of the self and others as part of a social system; the internalisation of authority and the assumption of responsibility for making explicit choices of ideology and lifestyle open the way for critically self-aware commitments in relationships and vocation.

Conjunctive faith (Early mid-life and beyond): The embrace of polarities in one's life, an alertness to paradox and the need for multiple interpretations of reality mark this stage. Symbol and story, metaphor and myth (from one's own traditions and other's) are newly appreciated (second or willed *naïveté*) as vehicles for expressing truth.

Universalisating faith (Mid-life and beyond): Beyond paradox and polarities, persons in this stage are grounded in a oneness with the power of being. Their visions and commitments free them for a passionate yet detached spending of the self in love, devoted to overcoming division, oppression and violence, and in effective anticipatory response to an inbreaking commonwealth of love and justice.

See Fowler: *Stages of Faith; Becoming Adult; Becoming Christian; Faith Development and Pastoral Care.*

3   *Young Church – Letter of Irish Bishops* (Veritas 1985).
4   *Dogmatic Constitution of the Church*: 5 c/f (4–12)
5   *Decree on Ecumenism.* 2/6.
6   See 'The Old Testament Message' in D. Bergeant *A Biblical Commentary on the Book of Job* (pp.16–20; 213–9).
7   St Paul Publications (1984).
8   Cf. *Lumen Gentium*, Ch 3.
9   *Ibid.*
10 *Love Is for Life* – Irish Bishops Pastoral, Veritas (1985). Cf. J. Dominion, *The Capacity to Love*, Darton, Longman & Todd.
11 *Ibid.*
12 *The Pope in Ireland*, Veritas (1979).

CHAPTER 2

A JOURNEY TO OPENNESS

I
EXPERIENCE AND DISCOVERY

I listen a lot to people who seem to know the truth. They open up their book of life and it's the most beautiful book of all. More often than not at this level of shared reflections on experience, feeling, thinking, deciding and doing their book is a real living gospel.

The people who had the most profound effect on me and were a real revelation were those who have left the Church – those who had instead joined 'house' Churches and who had a genuine meeting with Christ. They found him in together-ness, in solidarity of belonging, in sharing and in praying the scriptures. Christ was present to them also in the gentle, shared, silent praying moments. They could not find him in official Catholic ritual.

The other group were the 'Geldof' Christians — those who are great carers but do not 'practise' as ordinary Catholics understand it. A funeral liturgy at which I was present with a large gathering of this group was a most living worship. There was a real presence of Christ Jesus about it in the people who were present, in the music, the scripture, the silence, the com-passion and love for the dead colleague.

Is the call of God in such experiences? They connect with Bishop Donal Murray's challenge to the 1985 plenary assembly of the Secretariat for Non-believers in Rome.[1] His agenda for action indicated two main areas for the 'urgent work, crucial and decisive for the future of the faith in Ireland' spoken of by

Pope John Paul II at Maynooth in 1979. He says 'two main areas of weakness in Irish Catholicism which pose a threat for the future of the faith are:

    (i) the sense of community and of involvement is weak;

    (ii) the gospel vision is not sufficiently perceived as a source of hope, as speaking to every area of life and as providing each individual and the community as a whole with a mission.'

The Irish bishops' letter 'to all concerned with the pastoral care of young people' addressed the situation with even greater urgency. (See Chapter 1, section 3). They 'see a Church of Community and of Participation as *the* way of faith in the future'. Yet four of their 'six graced roads of discovering Jesus as Lord which we find *within* the Church' are largely overlooked. The adult Catholic community in the past concentrated its energy almost exclusively on two of these – Sunday mass and the sacraments. The young Church is much more responsive to the other four 'rich elements of our Catholic tradition' – belonging, service, scripture and silence.[2]

Bishop Michael Murphy of Cork has a specific vision for the 'parish and the challenge ahead'. A new style of leadership with renewed structures is necessary to perform the 'ongoing task' of building the Christian community. The challenge for each parish today, he says is, 'to utilise the talents of its members, to identify the needs of the community, and to harness the resources of the community to fulfil those needs'.[3] This participation and service are keys to overcoming a lack of conviction about the place of religion in people's lives.

Over twenty years ago I was very involved in a retreat movement by and for young people. The experience helped me to begin a process of striving to work with rather than for people. Its group approach also brought home the relevance of all that is outlined in Chapter 1:3 of *The Young Church*. Groups like the Priests Fraternity, Charismatics, Marriage Encounter, *Síol*, house meetings, group masses, scripture sharings confirm and reflect the significance of this approach.

In the 1970s time spent developing a professional approach
to leadership in a developmental group-work setting opened
the way to new discoveries. In collaboration with Leslie Button
of the University of Swansea and his colleagues we discovered
that forming and developing relationships of all kinds were
central to an educating process.[4] Research confirmed the way
that personality, environment, roles and norms shape our
beliefs, actions, attitudes, values, prejudices and responses. It
was then I began to realise that pastoral care demanded active
intervention in people's lives. Words like roles and norms,
peers became indications of subtle forms of social imprisonment, needing 'social diagnosis that is also social intervention'.

The core of youth work changed from activities to the development of the young person, from the structure of pastoral
care to the actual events that should make up a pastoral
occasion. We were taught some simple techniques for initiating
discussion and group action and for nurturing an affirmative
context that enabled us to spot deeper personal and social
needs requiring special attention. The freedom acquired by
young people from crippling self-concepts and from dominating social controls made it easy for them to connect to the
great themes of the gospel. Freedom, dignity and imaging of a
God who is a community of relationship was the outcome.

In our programmes of exploration of relationships, behaviour, the roots of feelings and the ingredients of true friendship
there was time for practising within the supportive context of
the group an appropriate social skill for each member. Then
following an outside experience which interlocked with the in-
group reflection and plan of action, the quality of the experience
deepened.

The most creative aspect of this programme was its effect
upon the group leader. A greater awareness of each member's
leadership capabilities led to a greater readiness to acquire an
active style. One soon saw the deep similarities between
permissive and authoritarian leadership. These can be very destructive where growth and development of the person,

autonomy of the individual, capacity to make free choices and social cohesion and utilisation of a diversity of skills, attitudes and ideas are our leadership objectives.

This focus on the person who is leader opened a new awareness. Real harmonious communion with others comes when we are most 'empty'. If I was stuck, not knowing where to turn, or if I decided to 'let go' after silent prayerful, sometimes painful, reflection nourished by scripture I seemed more open to the Spirit. Having heard an intimate put it 'as it is' or participated in groups with shared values reflecting a living witness (for example at anniversaries, marriages, baptisms, funerals) I modified my role. House and area masses, unity services for emigrants' welfare, pilgrimages, especially where the sick and young are present, all create community. Events with 'roots' – baptisms at holy wells, cemetery masses – the sharing with others in bereavement, anointing of the sick, employment action challenge entrenched norms. Celebrating achievements and successes of a family or community, as, for example, in sport, fundraising, youth musicals, parish drama and variety are other ways of bringing relationships to the fore as an educating process.

Yet acquiring an effective way of communicating demands more than common language. Making time for, listening to and learning from all who are ministers within the parish, recognising that people have both ideas and needs, is crucial. There is a need also to discover what is particular to individuals and what is common to all the people of the parish.

Many channels for contact and communication already exist in every parish. In addition to the Church ones, schools, sports clubs, voluntary groups, parent meetings are important openings for involvement. They create the space where laity willing to do something can plan, help and encourage each other to get started.

As community we grow in our understanding of what it is to be parish, letting go of old models of Church and inviting all to share responsibility – we evolve new ways of leadership.

This too calls for new kinds of decision-making. New structures begin to take shape.

II
THE WAY TO CO-RESPONSIBLE LEADERSHIP

The call to be parish is a call to be the body of Christ. By listening to and responding to the presence of the spirit in our lives, we work together in bringing the message of Christ alive. In helping to create a climate of warmth and acceptance, where the dignity of each person is accepted, we can help each other to grow and develop. We become the people God calls us to be.

But who tries to motivate people to work together in building up a vital Christian community? There is a variety of gifts and skills latent in the community. How are they fostered and given expression?

In our case we did it by providing leadership and co-responsibility. We gave people an opportunity to become involved in planning, decision-making and shaping the future of the parish. Our main method was through surveys and meetings. People had already been working together in the parish, in renovating the Church and schools as members of different organisations. There were also people involved in liturgy and school activities, field days and the like. They were invited to come together to provide consultation, advice and action.

From this came the establishment of the pastoral council. It brought a new era in the life of the parish. Those selected were immediately involved in planning and decision-making. To get a clear vision of its goals, the members of the pastoral council attended a meeting in Dublin with groups from other like-minded parishes. With them they searched for ways of promoting the faith in a changing society. Deepening our own spiritual lives was realised as a priority.

The delegates discovered that the ways people have practised their faith in the past are both a blessing and a problem. They inevitably influence their beliefs, values, attitudes and priorities. Our characters and personalities and their interaction with locally accepted norms and roles, have a powerful bearing on our ability to change. Often we have the will but not the freedom to make appropriate adjustments. Gradually to see all things in the light of faith, to judge and act always in this light, to improve and perfect oneself by working with others and in this manner to enter actively into the service of the Church, is much more a process of experience than of theory. Action and reflection need to go hand in hand.

In this matter the parish council members were disappointed that the newly elected National Conference of Priests did not offer the leadership in collaboration which had been provided by their predecessors.

However, in the parish every opportunity was availed of to bring people into the liturgy. People began to feel Christ present to them at significant moments of their lives. The existing prayer life and community spirit was our solid foundation. Popular traditional devotions, rosary and scripture prayer groups, novenas, eucharistic and Church pilgrimages and devotion at grottos were encouraged. Each opportunity was availed of for evangelising and faith development. The word of God was given special honour in preparation for the sacraments and in popular devotions. The readings of mass were explained daily. Homilies for all occasions especially funerals were on the word of God. There was occasional training of ministers of the word.

Experiences of involvement were given by the maximum possible participation in sacramental celebrations – first holy communion, penance, confirmation, marriage, as well as at liturgical events and funerals. We stressed the importance of the period from Easter to Pentecost, using readings from the Acts of the Apostles as illustrations of a caring Christian community.

Our schools played a major role, particularly in the sacraments classes. Parents were encouraged and helped by children, parish visitation and lectures to use their child's religion book for their own development in the faith. Children enjoyed reminding their parents of parental homework!

The parish pastoral council's work of unifying the fragmented and meeting the unmet was limited by time and by the voluntary nature of its membership. As the need for action intensified other groups and individuals were brought in. Leaders in these groups were encouraged and supported. Training was provided. Development groups within the community were given particular care and formation.

Training for and involvement in ministries has deepened the commitment to the Church of a number of lay people. Contact with other laity groups and involvement in courses, vigils and retreats was most valuable. Communication through bulletins, parish magazine, local newspaper notes and community radio was an important means of motivating people for greater involvement.

The clergy were constantly on the look-out for a variety of people who were willing to share a common search for 'the' vision, and prepared for an involvement of the Holy Spirit. Everyone was welcome. Each person is gifted. Some gifts are more rare than others. Often these are the ones most needed for building community. The accompanying 'Tree of Life' diagram shows many branches, twigs and leaves, as well as a deep rooted trunk. Leadership is at its heart. The branches, twigs and leaves are alive only to the extent that the people who motivate them are fed by the sap of the Spirit. Its roots are in the family of mankind, growing towards the universal family of God. The nurturing and pruning of this holy vine is the delicate task of the one and only true Father of us all, through the life-giving and gentle breath of his Spirit.[5]

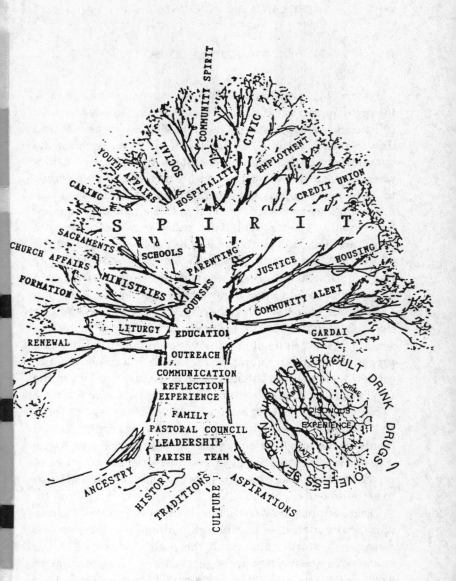

See Appendix 3, page 184

III
FORMING A TREE OF LIFE

Members of the parish who attended a one-year training course in parish ministry at St Patrick's Seminary in Carlow formed a parish team with priests and religious sisters. The growth and development of the parish could not happen without the commitment of this team. Its members are primarily action-orientated. Participation involves not merely allowing people to voice their opinions and describe their experiences but also the taking into account of their advice when the decisions are being made. 'Leaders who listen must be free enough from threat and fear, and confident enough in their God to let the whole story pour out ... a more challenging, perhaps a more painful but also a more honest way of being together.' Ben Kimmerling made these comments in September 1986 in a *Furrow* article at a time when the official Church was consulting the faithful in preparation for the Synod of the Laity. She had serious reservations about the value of consultation. The procedure offers no guarantee that the opinions sought and offered will be either listened to or taken into account in the final decision. 'Neither does it provide a comeback on a decision which proves to be unacceptable.' There is no mutuality or Christian equality. 'It's a procedure where control is kept firmly in the hands of one of the parties.' In contrast to the consultors freedom to act, the consulted party is only free to re-act, that is to accept or reject the invitation to participate or to accept the decision.

There is much to discredit this consultative procedure from episcopal appointments, through national commissions, to diocesan pastoral councils. If the reality is as bad as the evidence of priests and laity suggests the whole procedure, in Kimmerling's words, is 'a hollow formality or ritual carried out to conform to the letter of the law'.

There is little evidence at official Church level of any movement away from this meaningless consultation to real dialogue.

'If our leaders are to allow us to speak for ourselves they must be open to a radical change – in attitudes and in structures.' However, there is ample evidence from secular gatherings around the country that the days of tokenism are coming to an end.

It is a joy to visit places like Clogh – often the most rural of communities where simple but meaningful changes are radically reforming our way of being Church. Modern models of Church, thriving in such cultural diversity, are illuminating the defects of the hierarchical model that is beloved by so many of hierarchical status! It is hardly surprising then that in effect many of those life-giving models have not arrived by an official route. These changes came not from an official pastoral plan but by way of practical adventure at local level.

Our team strives to identify areas of need in the community, bringing surveys and consultation to a shared Christian reflection. It promotes the role of the laity, as servants of the fuller life of the Church. It provides the means necessary to integrate the faith we profess with our daily lives.

The team tries to create a climate within the community for the lay involvement outlined already. To promote and support the work of all our groups working for the Church and to help those involved to see its value in God's plan for their lives, the members use our Tree of Life as a visual aid to explain our parish structure and its meaning.

The tree is in our father's garden. It is rooted in Christ. The soil around its roots and trunk is our civil and religious society. Its deep roots reflect our traditions, ancestry, and values growing in the risen Christ. By means of the family, both domestic and ecumenical, and the civil society we emerge for a new beginning to love one another in a way informed by social action and justice.

Empowered by the life of Spirit the tree grows up into the clear, bright inviting heavens. It is sometimes touched by negativity and darkness as it grows. An occasional branch gets broken as it develops. The journey of growth and regrowth is nurtured by the parish pastoral council. The spirit of Christ is indwelling in all its branches and leaves. Reflection and evaluation is informed by the gospel in the main branches that lead on to the twigs. The animation by the leadership team is of particular importance here.

Interwoven through its growth and development is its spiritual significance which is nurtured by prayer and scripture study. The sap rises again through leadership and pastoral care to renew the work at the branch. At the back of every leaf (unseen by the naked eye!) are the little but significant words, why, how, what, where, when, who. So conversion is always necessary to enable each of us to do things for the right reason – love of Christ and the Church.

The team is in continuing formation. It does the homework for our pastoral council in an official way by co-ordinating the work of the various parish groups. It assists the members to act and interact as free and mature Christians. So much depends on the quality of leadership. Real growth requires that leaders work *with*, rather than *for*, those whom they wish to motivate for responsible action.

IV
WITH RATHER THAN *FOR*

The way in which community is built depends very much on the way its leaders work together. Growth depends on the way those who are in positions of authority or leadership in the parish work with people to foster the growth of a community feeling. All of us are living in community. Involvement in a parish means thinking of the parish as a community. Building the parish community is an ongoing process. It is something which we can never say that we have fully attained.

A beautiful new parish complex of buildings including a purpose-built community centre might still mean that people are isolated and lonely. The presence of many activities and groups does not necessarily indicate a real growing of community feeling among the people.

Church documents frequently see community as a geographical area, usually parish. When laity talk about community they signify the way people feel for other people. They speak in plain terms often using the word 'we' in describing what part they play in the lives of others.

Using expressions like 'trying to help them to live according to God's will', 'trying to help them to be holy' or even 'to live lives of love', are not concrete enough for most people. More human language is needed to explain the changes we are trying to bring about in the lives of people. So it is wise to think out what is hoped to be accomplished in individual lives. Veto on change has to be removed. Having considered our purpose, based on our beliefs, feelings and ideas then the moment for decision arrives. People lose interest if action does not follow *immediately*.

Our approach to working with people varies in different settings. Working *for* people procedures are based on the assumption that we know what people need: if they do what we say then this will be for their good. So we do all the thinking and planning for them. We have to use this approach with very young children. The problem here is how to get people to implement our ideas and decisions. It is an approach easy to use in schools, colleges, novitiates and seminaries – places where authority is respected. So there is a strong temptation to use the *for* method with people in the parish, if 'Father' is the boss. It is a model of leadership belonging to the past, most characteristic of authoritarian or fundamentalist Churches.

People who desire to work collaboratively *with* others but in their hearts are more committed to working *for* people, often use the most destructive of all styles of leadership, the permissive approach. This is a method which claims neither to help nor hinder people from taking whatever path they want to choose. Sometimes it is necessary – like the father of the prodigal son. There is always within a caring relationship, a time and a place for allowing things to happen. However, this is subtly different from the authoritarian style, which in desiring to be democratic, become permissive.

The way in which our parents and the other role models of our childhood exercised their authority moulds our own style of parenting. Leadership by diktat comes to us automatically from our conditioning. When we come to realise that such an approach is neither acceptable or effective we tend to let things happen. If then the consequences are not to our liking our feeling of being ultimately responsible causes our control mentality to break through in criticism, fault finding, judging and condemnation. Then conscious of proper gospel attitudes we become guilty about this response. We are tempted to opt out completely, our sense of accountability reminds us that we are responsible and we take unilateral decisions. This approach can clearly lead to confusion because it is in fact a more subtle and manipulative version of the authoritarian style.

If we are permitted to enter people's lives we cannot avoid influencing them. Our inescapable leadership is exercised by inactivity as much as by positive intervention. An authority relationship cannot be non-influencing. The permissive style is primarily destructive because it is mostly reactive, negative or critical and consequently destructive of community growth and development. Persons trapped in such a predicament have two options. They can either assume absolute rule on the style of the real authoritarian model or delegate leadership functions to others more capable of working in a collaborative way.

Experience has taught me that the extent to which I delegate the right to accept full responsibility to work *with* people in a collaborative style, the more I am allowing the group and its leaders share responsibility and accountability. Yet some have to be convinced that exercising leadership is not in itself authoritarian.

In the working with or collaborative style, structures of leadership are essential. The community or group is the primary reality. Authority comes much more from the service to the community than from the office. Authority, in addition to being decentralised, actually invites involvement challenging those who disrupt the process by inactivity.

The terms used to describe this style of leadership are 'encouraging', 'enabling', 'fostering', 'affirming', 'co-ordinating', 'leading to a relationship of partnership'. Authority based on service to the community fosters personal growth and benefits from the gifts and talents of all the members. It is not threatened by those members who are creative, imaginative or possessing the ability to innovate and experiment. Those more naturally gifted, when given space, tend to call forth the talents of others, raising awareness of both the needs and the riches of the community.

Where there is subservience, passivity or docility, often described by the paternalistic authority as loyalty, then the leadership is authoritarian. This is sometimes accompanied by an emphasis on the importance of the office, title, rank, seniority and honours, for example, monsignorship. Authority is centralised and dominant with power residing as an almost exclusive clerical possession.

Working *with* people helps them to listen to each other. It leads each one to grow and develop as a person, becoming more caring for other people. The community becomes more understanding and more tolerant. People grow in self-confidence. They make plans and carry them out. Partnership with participation becomes a reality. Our capacity for community involvement is often reflected in the attitude we bring to mass. The spirit of people's liturgical celebration is a barometer of our freedom from dependence.

V
FREED OF DEPENDENCE

The attitude we bring to mass says much about our image of ourselves, the Church and God. For many, mass still generates passivity. Their perception of the sacrifice is as recipients. Does this mentality reflect every aspect of our religious observance?

We live in a world educated to a belief in rising expectations. There is an expert or a service to minister to every need. The ethos and design of modern culture is to initiate us into the myth of a never-ending consumption of services. People are kept excited by 'sensations'. Otherwise they might start to think! Our cosmopolitan culture mistrusts two-way communication. Progress is real only where it is convertible into something tangible, that is consumable. This promised earthly paradise is the real opium of the people.

Our approach to the mass reveals our capacity to cope with such a culture. Our attitude to involvement indicates whether the eucharist is the 'source and summit' of our community and personal lives, as encouraged by Vatican II or something merely consumable.[6] Our attitude reveals if we still are slaves of mammon or have begun to lose our desire to be rich in things? Community leaders know that most learning comes from the freedom to reflect on and become involved in an activity that is meaningful. It is learning by doing and by discovering the significance of what is done. Our most important step to freedom is to transfer responsibility to ourselves and away from the instructor, bureaucrat, professional, or any outside institution or authority. We discover an opportunity to create and be recreated. We are freed of dependence on some master. We are discovering an alternative style of life.

Reality is never just the facts, laws or liturgical norms. It is also the individual person's story and perception. Is 'ordinary' too often perceived as 'inferior' in relation to the expert or 'superior'? Even when people or community discover that they have a right to a voice, they are led to believe that they need a professional to express it. Why should this be so? If people start reflecting and speaking for themselves they discover that they are engaged in an normal human act. This is a primordial human right. It is not just the privilege of a few, especially in the Christian community. Here all are equal in reflecting the image of God.

We too easily surrender our right to choose what we wish to say or do. Often that right is denied us in liturgy and Church life. When and how we express ourselves should not be at the mercy of the priorities and prejudices of those who come to us only as it suits their needs rather than ours. Communities that exercise the right of *self-expression* are more often a threat to the power of the dominating few than to the spirit of the gospel. Where power is the priority and tension inevitable, it must be dealt with in light of the gospel and the rights of the person.

There is little mention of the significance, nature and potential of community in public debate or the media. The needs of people within a local community as perceived by themselves and expressed by a medium under their own control threatens the liberal, dominating élite. Conversely, the national agenda can be very misleading. We have discovered a hunger in people for a medium to express themselves as they perceive themselves to be and reflect their views in the context in which they have been formulated. Community radio was born partly out of this hunger. The same hunger gives life to liturgical involvement. This is seen in the care taken by families in choosing symbols for the offertory procession for funeral masses and in the relevance of the homily and prayers of the faithful to the social context of the departed Christian's life.

Self-expression, participation, a sense of confidence and self-worth is as important to family and community fulfilment as it is to personality development. Intimacy, identification, the instant propagating of a caring philosophy and a pride in each others efforts calls for a freedom of a profoundly Christian kind. When we look at the lives of those who suffer from alienation we get some sense of what this freedom means for us. Alienation describes a reality where there are no feeling of belonging, no awareness of one's roots and origins, no vehicle to express one's ideals and culture, no opportunity to participate and create. Research consistently reveals that most 'delinquents' have difficulty with identity and involvement. No one accepts them, loves them or helps them to be in touch with reality. The

cosmopolitan culture subverts the insecure and sometimes
makes them violent. Its youth culture is often a voice of protest,
yet, sometimes of representation or remonstrance. They
become antagonists in our society, resentful even of legitimate
authority. There is no real dialogue between antagonists.
Community is violated. A Church of participation is a blessing
for society at the human as well as the spiritual level. We resist
most effectively the campaign to marginalise our Christian
influence by enabling people to be committed to creating
community. The deeper our caring the more the gospel will be
valued in society as a whole.

Most pagans admit that, 'We are to love one another, not to
be like Cain who belonged to the evil one and cut his brother's
throat' (1 John 3). In the Irish context the concept of voluntary
service expressing this Christian love is closely linked with
community development. If development is concerned with a
community helping itself, this implies voluntary service. It is
both good as a means and as an end in itself being a way of
living the call to love. It is also recognised, however, that there
are limits to voluntary service in the management and service
structure. Yet the greater the degree of voluntary involvement,
the more obvious is the spirit of the gospel. There is less risk
too of the professional becoming the master of the people. Only
by achieving the right to be itself and to assume its own voice
in the direction of its own destiny can a community be really
free. Professionals tend to rule out certain things by such
statements as: 'It is not up to standard', or 'What do they know
about liturgy?' One must check whether these norms were
formulated away from the core value and priorities of the
particular community. How can liturgy devised by strangers
celebrate the life in an active community?

Standards are necessary. People vary in self-awareness. An
inflated ego can sometimes blinker the accuracy of the view.
Reality as thought about does not always correspond with how
it is lived out in a social setting. Those who speak from thought
models, like academics and bureaucrats, may have a different

agenda than those who speak from experienced reality. Communities in our over-consuming and over-managed specialist society seldom hear the voice of reality. It is therefore essential that the liturgy group or parish pastoral council play a part in decision-making and planning. The structure should strive to enable the whole community to be its own master, hearing the cry and need of every heart. How else can we move towards a genuine collaborative priesthood?

1   D Murray, *Future of the Faith*, Veritas (1985).
2   *The Young Church* – A letter to all concerned with the pastoral care of young people, Veritas (International Youth Year, 1985).
3   M. Murphy, *The Challenge Ahead*, Cork Diocesan Office.
4   L. Button, *Developmental Group Work with Adolescents*, London University Press (1974).
     ————, *Discovery and Experience*, OUP (1971).
5   Clogh Parish Pastoral Team, *The Colliery Christians* (1992). This document indicates how the parish copes with financial affairs. Pages 40-41 detail the process of accountability under the supervision of the finance committee. Pages 2-12 consider the hurt and pain of unemployment and emigration and the parish programme to cope with them.
6   *Lumen Gentium* – Dogmatic Constitution on the Church II, AAS 57 (1965). See also John Paul II, 'On the Mystery and Worship of the Eucharist' (Holy Thursday, 1980).

CHAPTER 3

A COLLABORATIVE PRIESTHOOD

I
CREDIBILITY

A parish priest gets the canonical legitimacy he needs to exercise his role in the faith community by his appointment and installation. But to have credibility as a leader is much more difficult. A deal of human skill allied to spiritual authenticity is required to ask space, to take initiatives or hold up ideals to which we wish people to conform, especially if we inconvenience them by our expectations. A mere clericalist style of priesthood is no longer credible in the marketplace. Authenticity is crucial to the effective exercise of leadership. People nowadays want to unmask phoniness.

For a message to have credibility it must come from an authoritative source – from those perceived as knowing what they are talking about. It has to be publicly and officially proclaimed. It has to harmonise in some way with the needs, aspirations, values and dreams of those who are to be led by the message. If it is to eliminate barriers built by gender, status or social class, it must pose crucial questions, clarify how the issues harmonise with the core beliefs and then initiate action that realises the rhetoric.[1]

One of the crucial elements is to find the capacity to bridge the gap between public proclamation and individual action. The leader's own responsiveness is the crux of the matter. Yet the humble admission of our own limitations is not an obstacle to credibility. People are not too alarmed at the admission of some 'unchristian' practice in our religious tradition. A touch

of care, a willingness to relate, a word of consolation help when
the old answers ring hollow. We need to bring alive to those
who have been wounded by aspects of our religious tradition
by rejection or excommunication, for example, the presence of
a loving Christ, by encouraging them to trust in their own
religious experience. Our first priority should be a willingness
to help them interpret their experience of life in a wider, deeper
and more meaningful context.

A life-giving faith in Jesus comes by the way of love. People
get angry when we speak of the abundance of God's grace and
then proceed to make it scarce by ecclesiastical regulation. Why,
for example, is there more genuine reconciliation through AA,
Gamblers Anonymous, counselling, therapy support groups
and retreat houses than in going to confession.

It is difficult to take ownership of the wrong things in our
life. An experience of *unconditional* love, where the dark side
is known and yet forgiven, opens the door to self acceptance,
especially in the self-centred and sinful areas. It is in the presence of love that we can recognise our personal powerlessness.
Unconditional love enables us to see our lives and relationships
more clearly and in context. We priests have been trained to
be in control. To face reality we need to look at the attitudes,
roles and norms that shape our experience and performance
even in confession!

The sacrament of penance/reconciliation is a real symbol
for the people of the priest's leadership style.[2] Pre-conciliar
confessional practice is often seen as the most potent aspect of
the control model. Many people see confession as the Church
laying guilt – and even shame – upon them. True conversion
comes from within; from a clear commitment to the truth, from
an ability and willingness to name the core of our problem.
People want a sacrament which is a process of reconciliation,
helping them to hold in tandem the indwelling Spirit, and the
God without, who is our father. For conversion we need
strength too from the God outside the self. It is this God who
finally unfolds in us the knowledge that we are not just sinners,

addicts, compulsives and complete victims of darkness and doubt. We are also his children, redeemed by Jesus, staying with the pain and darkness, his father raised him from death. It is his Spirit who calls us into a loving community where, standing with each other, we learn to stand alone. Here too, we are called to serve and touch others in their pain.

When we own our brokenness and can tell others of how we have been raised up, is not this a credible witness to the death and resurrection of Christ? Are we not then real sponsors of each other? We are mentors, sisters and brothers with no concern for class, age, status, philosophy, hierarchy, race or even religion, but carers with equal vulnerability. The sin, even in those with great responsibility, is brought to Christ not in condemnation but in love.

Our parish experience of the sacrament of reconciliation is very positive. People delight in meeting the healing, consoling, forgiving, Christ at whatever point they are in the journey of becoming whole. While confession evokes the negative, the experience of unconditional love and acceptance ultimately frees people to tell their real story. Since we have moved the focus of reconciliation from confession to a public and comm-unity celebration of God's mercy, people feel less deprived of the abundance of God's grace.

A clericalist Church constantly loses credibility by the way in which it seems to limit the abundance of God's grace. Do we not limit the abundance of God's grace in maintaining a worldwide scarcity of prophets, shepherds, and ministers of the word and sacrament, by refusing to ordain married people or women to the priesthood? We further limit it by giving a second-class status to the praying, caring, helping, healing, reconciling, enabling, affirming, guiding ministries provided by religious and laity. People, especially priests who believe this is true, lose their credibility when they suppress such con-victions. A spiritually integrated and honest person has far more authenticity in the field of leadership than the defender of the institutional view.

There are human factors also. The priest as leader has to be open to discussion and negotiation about how leadership is to be exercised. Knowledge of the non-negotiables is also crucial; official parish policy cannot be contrary to the gospel, especially the law of love. Relationships that are nurturing and freedom-granting surpass those based on status, role, duties and appearance. Open sharing of feelings is far more effective than competiveness. A style of leadership that pulls rank and puts emphasis on the power of the office contradicts the teaching of Jesus. On the other hand inviting involvement, sharing authority and responsibility, co-ordinating a great variety of charisms and functions fosters good working relationships, evokes support and lessens the burden of leadership. An authority which is dominant and centralised works against the growth of personal and Christian maturity and promotes mere docility and passivity and fosters alienation.

We need companions to walk with us on the way of Christ if we are not to get lost in the wilderness of our secular, media-massaged, sensationalist society. Some of our most helpful companions are the members of other Christian denominations. Their collaboration is essential if we are to be truly committed to the will of Christ for his followers. In spite of our diversity it is possible to reflect something of the unity for which Christ prayed to his father.

II
IN ONE CHRISTIAN COMMUNITY

My class piece proclaims *Ut Omnes Unum Sint*.[3] The centre piece shows Paul VI embracing Patriarch Athenagoras of the Eastern Orthodox Church. This breach of the boundary of division after 1,000 years caught our imagination. From the time of the deathbed unity prayer of John XXIII to this historic meeting in the Holy Land in the year of our ordination, the Vatican II of unity fired our ideals and stimulated us. We saw Christ's death

wish for unity as the essence of our call. Our desire for Christian
unity sprang from a need to be faithful to God's will. On it
depended the credibility of our witness. 'So that the world may
believe' (John 17: 21) was precisely Christ's prayer for unity in
his final address to the world.

Our priority in the parish is to strengthen the union we have
in Christ and to be his community. Whatever we can do together we do. We regard ourselves as one community with three
places of worship – one Church of Ireland and two Roman
Catholic. It is our policy to give public expression to that union
which we share. We have an ever-increasing respect for each
other's teachings, understandings and practice. We share
common creeds and draw our belief from the same word of
God. We acknowledge that, through the death and resurrection
of Christ, we are delivered from the power of Satan and sin,
Jesus saves us from guilt, alienation, estrangement from God,
moral corruption, self-centredness and death. We see incorpor-
ation into the freedom of Christ through baptism as the path
to human fulfilment and sincere service of neighbour. We know
that in its deepest reality the Church is much more invisible
than visible. It is Christ – risen and present.

We see the visible Church as community and the way people
relate to and care for one another. This flows from our relationship with God, rather than from an institution directed from
above by legal norms. We are working for structures, norms
and systems that spring from and are rooted in the values of
the local Christian community. We hold it important that
people believe in their own dignity as children of God and to
feel precious in his sight. Each of us is put into this world to
make a unique contribution.

Women, the young, the marginalised, and fellow Christians
will find an equal place in the Church by our creation of community and making right relationships within it the focus of our
attention and energy. The only way we have of understanding
God's love for us and our preciousness to him is when we are
shown it by the significant people in the Church visible. That

is why the freedom to live right relationships with ourselves, with others, with the environment and with God is the cornerstone and basis of our shared unity.

Each community has a need to respect its history and traditions. Good values and relationships are malleable substances. They, like the cement in the building that binds all, keep us together as a Christian community faithful to tradition but open to the change necessary for growth and renewal. Our core value is charity inspired by faith in the risen Christ.

We are not so much called to give charity as to live it. We strive to give the suffering and needy a significant place. Jesus gave a significant place to the non-significant, like the woman taken in adultery or the woman at the well who was of the wrong creed. Jesus gave women and all the marginalised their rightful place in the community.

Respect should be the key word in all our attitudes. More than 500 people of both denominations shared recently in a Way of the Cross on Good Friday from the Colliery Church of Ireland Church to the Sacred Heard Church in Moneenroe, both in Clogh parish. It was acknowledged as the most moving of Good Friday liturgies – perhaps because the great variety of bearers of the cross from station to station were living that experience in their daily lives.

The Church continues and extends the mission of Christ, by accepting his command to be his witness in the power of the Spirit, in the service of love. Fulfilling this mission, doing separately only what conscience will not permit us to do together, is an expression of our commitment to the plan of God.

Areas of common witness include acknowledging how much there is in each other's manifestations of Christian faith and life that we can appreciate. We seek each other's trust and co-operation, for example in community service, in the use of media, in fresh thought and action about the urgent social issues, in speaking the truth in love. We pray together as family in solidarity and friendship, at all significant community events.

As one community and in solidarity, companionship and

respect for their religious tradition, we shared with the Church
of Ireland in rededicating their Colliery Church. Together we
offer a deeper vision through scripture as Jesus did, for example
the disciples on the road to Emmaus (Luke 24: 13-35). We each
avoid rushing in with our 'truth'. We assist fellow Christians
to see the rich variety of ways Jesus can be encountered in their
own living tradition. In this way there is a more careful human
and companionable journey of searching, with greater sensitivity to each other's spiritual roots. We have a genuine respect
for each other's freedom to go further on the road to faith, even
with the faltering steps of Peter where necessary.

We agree that the work of the Church in proclaiming
Christ's incarnation and saving mission includes an invitation
to respond. We call it renewal/conversion. In making our response we depend on the gift of God by whose grace we are
saved through faith. Each human person's response depends
on the Blessed Trinity. It is the father who gives his supreme
gift to his son, Jesus Christ, for the life of the world. It is the
Holy Spirit who opens our minds and hearts to accept and
proclaim that Jesus Christ is lord. The Holy Spirit guarantees
that the salvation which the father brought to fulfilment in
Jesus Christ becomes effective in each of us in a personal way
and is lived out in a social context. Those beliefs are common
to us. There is also a considerable consensus among us that
repentance and faith, conversion and baptism, renewal and
growth in the Christian community all belong together. We
differ about their place or priority in the scheme of salvation.

The whole movement of the call of God and our response
is illustrated in the process of coming to full faith. The journey
begins for us with baptism. At our first interdenominational
celebration of Holy Week we lit our Pascal vigil fire at the traditional site of the area's first Church. We carried the flame to
light the fire at the Church on the thirteenth century site and
then on to the modern site. The young were particularly
excited. The use of the water brought from St Patrick's Well as
Easter water and the bringing of the water by the parish priest

for the Easter baptism at the Colliery Church found a positive response from young and old, Catholic and Protestant. The common scripture of the event stressed unity as a fruit and agent of the gospel. The Church, the gospel and unity belong together.

Stimulated with a mission to return to others in our own Church, to share what we experienced, we were shapers of our own future, channels of the Spirit. We were shaping the future of the Church. Within and through it, we came closer to that unity which is at the heart of Christ's prayer for his faithful.

It is in this spirit that we work together. We write joint messages and pastorals for major feasts and events. We address human problems together: in setting up an ecumenical temperance movement – praying 'one day at a time' – for a specified period. Employment action and housing programmes, parties for the elderly, support for the bereaved and emigrants are offered on a single Christian community basis. We support each other's events – spiritual, social and financial.

Our work together makes demands on each other's trust. We have pointed out the risks of attendance at fundamentalist events in a fourth Church in the parish. It is no service to the gospel, ecumenism or evangelism to allow people to be drawn into group Churches that are not completely committed to encouraging their fellow Christians to be faithful to their own tradition. True ecumenism is built on respect and trust. We encourage fellow Christians to be converted anew by discovering the rich diversity of their own tradition. We refrain from comparing the misunderstood elements in our sister Christian Church with the best in ours.

If we truly believe in what Jesus teaches us about ourselves and others, if we have the permission of our community to live it, then true evangelisation is as inevitable as light after darkness. A Christian community striving to live as Christ prayed for it affirms each person as beloved of God. We become more like Jesus, seeing ourselves as pleasing to the father (cf. Luke 22) and as caring for the rejected and the marginalised.

Dialogue and open communication keep us together in our work for ecumenism. It is only when we let go of our pre-conceived notions of one another that we grow and pray in unity. We find a new way to Christ as brothers and sisters.

III
RELATING IN A NEW WAY

The journey of discovering with parishioners the difference between clericalism and priestliness is an exhilarating and freeing one. At this time in an Ireland of alienation and fragmentation caused by the collision of past and future, community and participation is both possible and desirable. At a time when clericalism and sacredness of status and role are diminishing, priesthood imbedded in the *Pobal Dé* – the priestly people – is being renewed and the role transformed.

The US bishops told the Synod on the Laity that the Church is in search of a new symbolic and effective system that helps us to imagine and listen to God in our life. The priesthood is the crucible of that search. So it is both an exhilarating and painful time to be a priest. Many of our thinking people are very uncomfortable with the hierarchical/institutional model of Church and its accompanying vision of ministry. They refuse to be treated like children. Delight at doing what 'father' says is going.

Lay involvement has now reached the stage comparable to adolescence in human development. Even our childlike perception, our idealised view of mother Church is tarnished. This can be emotionally upsetting. The strings and pulls of independence bring tension. There is the surge of energy, the struggle for identity and more independence. There is threat – which leads to conflict, fight or flight. Roles more appropriate to children lose their attractiveness. There is a peaking of desire for a more independent involvement and fuller participation. Desire for an effective share in decision-making causes parent care to be seen more as control than as love. Families, industry, voluntary organisations, many new religious and other groups without a rigid authoritarian structure have found a more modern way to perform. Through the experience of daily living, more adult ways of holding each other accountable have evolved. Role changes are part of surviving in the market place. The recent assertiveness of 'the women of Ireland' is a catalyst of the new order.

The growth of an adult Church demands more than a theme, a task or a plan. Women in particular focus on the relationships, demanding self-disclosure and the taking of life-giving risks. Community is bonded by relationships. Many men are happy putting order on the tasks and desire to 'get on with it'. Womenfolk search for the meaning, the purpose, the reason, the value and what's in the mind of the doer as they 'get on with it'.

In consequence, the priest has to relate to his people in a new way that is often devoid of the protection formerly afforded by the boundaries established by his role. He is more in need of the truth that only a friend can give. He now has to learn how to be affectively responsive and responsible. We need to be sure enough of ourselves and confident enough of our ability to allow another person to come close enough so that we too can be changed by the relationship. The very notion of self (and the threat of some loss of self) calls for an ability to explore options – particularly when in times of crisis. The maturing need of self-disclosure has to be balanced by selectivity and caution. So priests have many colleagues but few intimates.

Since the appropriateness of behaviour, especially in sharing wounded and vulnerable moments, is learned rather than taught, a renewal course is most valuable to clarify experience. My participation in a course organised by the National Conference of Priests of Ireland – the priests' representative body – was an excellent experience for me personally. There are also valuable insights to be gleaned from the published papers and tapes of their more recent annual congresses.

Valuable too is the Summer Institute for Priests in Seton Hall University, South Orange, New Jersey, USA. All have helped to transform and set me free.

In the earlier years of our priesthood we are still at the age when we have the ability to reflect, to journey into the spirit of obedience, poverty, and chastity. We are capable of change and growth. In practice we discover on whom or what we set our hearts and will. Is not this a radical spiritual question? It cannot be answered if we do not know self or are not confident enough to disclose its deeper aspects. With whom do we share the questions: Where am I going? Who am I besides being a priest? Who cares if I died, left the priesthood or used my energies in another way? It is with a sense of guilt we ask, what do I really want for myself. If I do not know what to give, how can I give it in a relational way? What do I know of my buried experiences that shape my personal and pastoral responses and reactions? When I experience my own brokenness and feel the need to be redeemed is it by a thing or a person? If I don't trust my senses, how do I validate my feelings? Do I survive by avoidance? Do I survive by being a thing? Do the things of God replace my relationship with a person – Jesus, Son of God?

In the past celibate love was distant, caring, avoiding involvement by ritual, rule and role. Our love was universal, carefully avoiding the day-to-day give-and-take of a concrete love, with particular persons. Today's quest for meaning and intimacy demands a quality of relationship which inspires, empowers and affirms those with whom we relate. Plunging ourselves into the mystery of love is both a precarious frontier and a divine calling. Being everyone's friend is both a road to burn-out and loss of our identity. A sense of subtle flirtation can lead to self-rejection or a rejection of sexuality. We need to think about those who help our maturing process – those who help us cope with our fears, emotions and our shifting image of ourselves.

In assisting others to assess their real motivation we need to be able to read our own. If we rationalise or get angry, who gets hurt? Do we struggle for separateness or togetherness, to control or to free, to intellectualise or to feel, to stay or run? The person we are is central to our pastoral role. It is as men that we are called to be priests. If our manhood gets lost in a clericalist role, is Christ's priesthood also crushed?

People accept our love best when we do good out of awareness of our vulnerability and brokenness, rooted in and rejoicing in God's mercy. If it is merely unconsciously doing good to make up for the bad in us people sense self-hatred, self-preoccupation and a lack of fidelity. It is particularly obvious if we are threatened by equals. We are happier with those 'below' us – the suffering and helpless. So our prayer to the lord to grant us a pure heart is not merely about chastity. It has pastoral and personal implications.

However, we are also men called to love and serve as representatives of the Church. A renewed priesthood also calls for a renewed Church. A renewed style of leadership by the priests also calls for a renewed way of leadership for the Church itself.

A pastoral plan that fails to take account of the importance of relating in this new way could be a disservice to renewal. Any plan that hasn't grown out of the total experience of being Church at local level could hardly be pastoral. In the absence of a renewed way of leadership for the Church itself pastoral planning is best left to local initiative. Active encouragement for the principles of the Ryan report with total freedom for local initiative could provide the foundation stone for an evolving national plan.[4] Meanwhile the legal priorities of the clerical official Church might be given a ten-year sabbatical.

In furthering the simultaneous renewal of person and structure the Christian Churches might actively support the evolution of communities with an ethos and practice similar to the experiences recorded here. Because of the primacy of obedience in Roman Catholicism it is particularly urgent for authorities at every level in our Church to alter radically the way authority is exercised. Crucial to this is the way in which its leaders are chosen, their faith confirmed and appointed to the ministry and apostleship of witnessing to the resurrection.[5].

Fifteen years of statements and resolutions from the annual and regional conferences of the NCPI provide splendid guidance in the matter for the authorities at home and in the Vatican.[6] Perhaps a brief reflection on the obstacles to a renewed Church at the level from which leadership in renewal is expected might open the door to more effective pastoral planning. Models of Church where space for creativity is a priority will be obstructed where those who want absolute authority residing high up in the structure also retain absolute power. Renewal by permit from personalities hostile to the process that brings it about is an impossibility.

IV
IN A RENEWED CHURCH

The whole social context of the priesthood is changing radically. Yet the 'old wineskins' of the institutional Church and the legal priorities of the clerical official Church could be increasingly inhibiting the maturing process of the new wine. The role of authority in particular must be assessed if we are effectively to 'reflect on our present reality'. This is not merely a question of the personal relationship between priest and bishop or priest and people. All are imprisoned by the legal – authoritarian aspects of the Church as a society.

The priest is at the cutting edge of where real change takes place in the Christian community. Pondering the conflicting demands being made on his ministry could be the means with which to reveal many hidden realities, especially 'inbuilt' conflicts within the Church itself.

The new priest during the rite of ordination gets a perception of his role as dispenser of sacred mysteries. Does this perception, combined with his training to be an idealistic teacher, undervalue the way his message ought to be learned, presented and lived? More crucially does it leave the christian community with a teaching president but without a leader?

The official rule book that guides his pastoral responsibilities – the Code of Canon Law – in reality merely communicates a hierarchical dimension. Official power is given more authority than a community's experience of the Spirit. The highest office holder is expected to evaluate organisational matters of which he had no personal experience. If priests feel like this how do the laity feel. And what about the groups who perceive themselves as marginalised: women, the young, the poor? Do we not claim that they too have received the gift of the Spirit? Vatican II acknowledged that the Church is both hierarchical and charismatic.[7] In our hierarchical Church, creating community, co-responsibility, and a 'secure environment', involves the priest's relationship and dialogue with his own authority. Awareness of how each priest comes to understand his role and how he exercises it is crucial if the role is not to be merely cultic or organisational. At the core is our response to the call of love as priest and people see it together.

Because of many modern competing demands and conflicting priorities placed before him by the people and the Church, it is easy for the priest to retreat into a life of sacramental duties and unavoidable committee work. Helping people to grow is an essential task but it is slow, tedious and time-consuming.

Many priests feel that appointment procedures do little to further the process by which a Church of communion and participation is created.[8] Should priests who are part of this process be moved out at the unexpected stroke of the bishop's pen? Creating expectations that are merely a notional concern of authority only leads to frustration and discouragement. It is the experience of such frustration that leads to calls for a national pastoral plan.

People's expectations and the reality of his situation tend to make the priest a multi-purpose community leader. Yet at the core he is trying to involve people in doing things for themselves. He has to build within them the capacity to do this by providing them with the necessary human and technical skills. This involves creating a self-awareness that reflects a view of their own strengths and weaknesses. They need to discover and deal with the constraints that surround them and the way in which their own attitudes and feelings impinge upon the exercise of the human skills needed. It takes time to provide appropriate supportive structures for the ongoing exercise of these skills in an increasingly autonomous way. People have to be encouraged to reveal their innate fears at every step, for practice in and reflection on the skills they are trying to acquire. What style of pastoral plan is needed to address these very essential elements? Such a plan must take into account that growth in self-awareness and social competence must be built into activities, programmes and social contacts. They interact in some way like this:

| Activities | Preparing for | I feel |
| Social Contacts | Reflecting on | I hope |

Creative leadership engenders a system that will contain a pattern of vigorous reinforcement of human and social skills exercised in their institutional context. Each aspect should contribute to helping clergy and parish workers to know their potential. If we underline their strengths we improve their self-esteem. If we help people reveal innate fears we ought to respond to the revealed fear. Each activity should have an inbuilt human/social contact. If we create a little capacity for thinking we are growing towards a cognitive rather than a total affective response. We are also removing emotional obstacles to action. An agreed plan emerging from a theoretical framework could be an obstacle to necessary change in the hands of an authoritarian leader.

Risk-taking is the essence of change. Those of elevated status often feel that failure will lead to loss of face. The true dignity of the human is best discovered by a holy communion with Christ present in his people who suffered the indignity of the cross. Unity in essentials, while allowing for the maximum self-governance at the basic Christian community level, presupposes trial and error. The discipline provided by the scripture and the essential principles drawn from Christian lives and the traditions of the Church will always restore us to his way. If any person is to be the ultimate adjudicator then it should be Christ the head. Otherwise everything should be evaluated through dialogue and in the light of the gospel.

If dialogue is to be honest, relevant and constructive, it is important that evaluation of the expectations and perspectives from 'above' must be sought and encouraged. None of us should take too personally the discovery that not everyone sees it the way we do. Those with the most power must be the first to give genuine trusting and practical recognition to the importance of the presence of the spirit of wisdom and truth in the heart of God's people. When they gather in his name to discern his will in the light of their experience and prayer, the authorities' perspective may sometimes be irrelevant! But it is so hard to let go of control when we are ultimately responsible.

As a beginning in dialogue imposing one's view on another should officially be recognised as a significant sin, no matter how exalted we may feel the office to be. Is it not real sin to stunt growth in myself or another? Dialogue must permit the possibility of changing the authority's perspective, even if it is enshrined in the Code of Canon Law. Our changing world demands a permanent inspiration for change.

In response to today's alienation the priest, as the authority in a parish, is expected to create a Church of communion and participation with dialogue and co-responsibility. Theologians tell us of several models of Church through which the dignity of every vocation is to be recognised. The fullness of life is expected to be a growth process. This is unlikely to be organically complete if the model of Church based on a mere legal code takes priority. If all the significant decisions are to be made 'high up' – away from the experience and reflection which give relevance and authenticity – how can people be motivated for participation, personal responsibility or creative involvement?

The attitude with which we approach our pastoral mission is crucial. Twenty-five years ago when we began implementing Vatican II, Catholicism re-focused on the 'good news' of the gospel. The mentality, values, and attitudes of Church directives are too often seen to be built around the 'bad news' of our untrustworthiness and natural inclination to evil. Is this the unspoken justification of the authoritarian style?

Such a mentality does not build self-esteem and the capacity for self-direction which arises from it. It deepens the alienation felt by an ever-increasing number of people, resentful of authority, imposed views and actions. Where the morale of clergy is low this is often the primary (though hidden) reason.

A community that is Spirit-guided ought to be able to emulate the way authority is exercised within family and civil society. The unpredictability and diversity of human personalities and their 'colour' in thoughts, actions, conversations, friendships are not a negation of the image of God in which they are made. Variety is the spice of life. It is also the gift of the Spirit. The fear of God is only one of his seven gifts. The exercise of the other six may be a more urgent priority for this time of change.

V
OPEN TO THE SPIRIT

Traditional Irish homes deeply ingrained in us the importance of prayer, fear of God and a sense of sin. Life was the vale of tears where we 'poor banished children of Eve' struggled through the eye of an needle to get to Heaven. The truths of our religion had to be learned in an exact form. We were 'little heretics' if we did not know in systematic order, prayers, creeds, commandments and sacraments. To be unfaithful to our religious duties, and to the ten commandments was *the* disaster. Our young lives were a daily reminder of the importance of the 'faith'.

'God will punish you.' We heard that so often. We were constantly reminded that God saw everything. We had to be good to please him. Our austere parish priest often examined us in school. He reinforced the idea of a severe God, by constantly calling for his blackthorn. He put the 'fear of God' in us! In our seminary years, the demand, 'Give me the words that are in the book' reinforced the centrality of orthodoxy as fundamental to faith. Everything was revealed by God. The Church infallibly knew God's mind. Dare we question one iota!

Authority too shared in that infallibility. Conformity to its rules and regulations was not only God's will for us, it was *the* sign of our vocation. From obeying the first tone of the bell, to how we carried our biretta in liturgical procession, our role was regulated. The way to holiness was by subservience to authority, moral observance and total conformity to the minutiae of seminary rules. 'Singularity' was a major obstacle to receiving holy orders. Space for the action of the Holy Spirit was limited by regulation and the fear of punishment resulting from their violation. There were rewards too for conformity.

Yet the wonderful tones of the *Veni Creator Spiritus* at ordinations and at the opening of our retreats did acknowledge the work of the Spirit.[9] It is through the Spirit that we can cry, 'Abba, Father'. The Spirit too is our teacher. He illuminates our minds to see what God reveals in Christ in whom revelation reached its completion. But learning this took much time and effort and the providential guidance of the Lord, for many years after ordination.

During the late 1970s and early 1980s involvement with charismatic renewal had a considerable influence on my personal faith development. From the late 1960s I had attained much experience in working with youth ministry groups. One group in particular, called the Christian Living Exercise group, was a junior version of the Cursillo movement – both of which were retreat movements that placed considerable emphasis on the role of the laity in the mission of the Church.

It had five elements: (a) a sense of welcome and belonging was actively fostered; (b) a sense of mission was promoted with young people, especially those over seventeen-years old, inviting other young people to share in a weekend retreat; (c) the talks on the weekend were sharings by youth to youth mostly on faith and life themes; (d) prayer, scripture and liturgy were at the heart of the experience; (e) getting to know Jesus and to live his Love was reinforced by a weekly discussion and liturgy in a hospital for the elderly as a reminder of needs outside the group. The new members were then introduced to the spirit of welcoming and mission, bringing other young people through the same five elements.

The formation and education took place in the context of the apostolic outreach of each individual. When we had an outreach as a group it developed. When timidity and intro-spection took over we diminished. The young priests and religious involved played a vital role in active leadership, motivating the youth to go beyond their fears and insecurity and invite other youth to come and meet Jesus. We ourselves were still searching for a social and spiritual identity. We received much help in our own vulnerability especially in the area of human relationships and the hunger for intimacy.

There was, however, a missing dimension. Our testing, evaluating, and discerning sometimes brought doubt rather than faith. The realisation dawned that without the Spirit, spiritual staleness rather than life in Christ was our witness. How could the old faith be always new and fresh, of the heart as well as of the lips (Cf. Mark 7)? We all have to be 'born anew', 'born of the spirit' (Cf. John 3). 'A new heart I will give you and a new spirit I will put within you …'(Ezek. 36). This will result in 'love, joy, peace, patience, kindness, goodness, fidelity, gentleness and self control'. These are all attitudes and actions which the Holy Spirit himself produces. But how does this happen to me or rather in me as my nature seemed to resist these fruits.

Our call to holiness is a process of producing these fruits of the Spirit. It is through the Spirit we 'abide in Jesus' (cf: John 15). Holiness is the expression of the Christ life from within. Our seminary holiness encouraged lives of quiet desperation and 'trying to be good' – struggling for salvation by merit rather than mercy. Our five elements (above) continued to have much of this seminary mentality.

A great sense of our spiritual bankruptcy was not a legacy of upbringing and seminary training. Is not the moral life more a fruit of the Spirit, than the means of holiness? This was the question arising from our weekly scripture sharing. We began to discover that forgiveness, a pure heart, a sense of justice, a hospitable home, reciprocal love and other expressions of moral and social renewal primarily came from prayer and interior surrender to the Spirit. The exercise of authority, conformity to rule, the enforcement of law are not the primary contributors to coping with 'all these evil things' (which) 'come from within' (cf: Mark 7), threatening my continuance in the priesthood. The emptiness began to provide space for the Spirit.

The demands of love are more exciting than the demands of the law. However, in Christ Jesus and through promptings of the Spirit, what is not possible for our weak nature becomes possible to God. In my parish environment where people were affected by social injustice, discrimination, bad health and inadequate housing, poor food, inadequate employment, I lacked real compassion to motivate me to do something about such injustice and the causes of evil. It is so easy to opt out.

True compassion comes from prayer. It leads us to Jesus and his compassion, his suffering with broken humanity. Priests have a daily contact with rich nourishment for prayer in the daily mass. The sentiments of the breviary provided me with abundant material for centring in Christ. It was in this milieu that the involvement in the charismatic renewal movement helped me to let the Spirit do it.

Participation in three priests' retreats run by the CRM

deepened my faith and healed much of the brokenness within. Yet it was reflecting and sharing during two retreats directed by Fr Ed Farrell that I discovered how to let the Spirit's life lead. We were reflecting on advice given to him by Mother Teresa of Calcutta on giving a holy hour. She told him, 'Let Jesus do it' and had nothing further to add.

That experience has been very helpful in the journey from merely saying prayers to real prayer. Its focus on scripture and on understanding the diversity of gifts and how to discern each person's unique charism was both a model of Church and an encouragement of pastoral planning.

We had to take time and space to make God and his will as the first of our priorities. When there is not much joy in the doing of a task and when there seems to be little contact was the time when our whole community discovered together that only God can console. God is so often revealed in a shared religious experience and seems so elusive in text and theology books! Ask those who have attended so many traumatic funerals, especially of the children and young adults, in our community in the past five years. All our holy hours are conducted in the Spirit and many of our other devotions. We try to let 'Jesus do it' risking ourselves to his inspiration.

A vital, worshipping, faith-filled community is a real support to the prayer and faith of the priest. The adoration, praise, thanksgiving and petition offered by the whole people, willingly assembled and actively involved, has profoundly touched this priest. Nowhere is this more obvious than at Christmas and Holy Week but it is felt throughout all life's milestones (sacraments and pilgrim resting posts) or in journeying back to our roots (at holy wells) and right to journey's end, as celebrated at cemetery masses or in funeral liturgies.

All of these events and in particular our parish mission had several aspects of the five elements mentioned above. Yet something more was needed to create a deeper awareness of the essential action of the Holy Spirit to bring renewal and change. Our Seminar in the Spirit in the spring of 1993 together with the Faith Friends programme touched many in a way that pointed us towards real renewal. Connecting our lives to the transforming power of the Spirit convinces even those of inadequate faith, of the truth and relevance of the Gospel.

Sanctifying the major moments and experience of life is particularly important to the broken and the poor. People want priests especially to build a bridge from their messy world to God. Our lay visionaries too are in constant need. The *unconditional* love of Jesus taking precedence over sin and struggle, touches the most fearful and isolated, encourages sharing at his table. We are led to renewed awareness of God and are renewed in his image.

---

1   J. D. Halloran, (Director, Centre for Mass Communications), 'Attitude Formation and Change', Television Research Committee, Working Paper No. 2, Leicester University Press (1967).

2   See Chapter 6, Section 4.

3   A class piece is a picture showing the individual photographs of a class. The one in question shows those priests who were ordained in St Kieran's College, Kilkenny in 1964. The motto *Ut unum sint* means 'that they may be one' (John 17: 21).

4   NCPI (National Conference of Priests of Ireland) report under the chairmanship of Bishop L. Ryan (1990). It established the need for the simultaneous renewal of personnel and structures and suggested means of procedure.

5   Acts 1: 26.

6   A council and executive is elected every three years by all the priests of Ireland to represent their concerns within the Irish church

7   See *Dogmatic Constitution on the Church*, Sections 10–12; 18–22.

8   See the splendid statement issued by NCPI (*Intercom*, Nov 1987) which brought a reprimand from the Papal Nuncio. Cf. M. O'Carroll, 'Has the Priesthood Been Devalued?' *The Furrow* (July 1987).

9   A classic hymn to the Holy Spirit.

CHAPTER 4

A NEW AWARENESS OF GOD

I
RENEWS IN HIS IMAGE

Our model for prayer is the relationship between Jesus and his father. That relationship of infinite love is a person and the Spirit. That Spirit is God's 'first gift to those who believe'.[1] He is praying in us, even when we are not aware of it.

Our prayer is a journey into an awareness of where God is present in our lives. There are privileged places of revelation of his presence. We meet God in people – in their stories, in their sense of God. We meet him in certain events in life – at times of healing or reconciliation or repentance, or at the moment we recognise that we have been given the power to do what we had relinquished into his hands. We meet him in a moment of peaceful communion with the magnificence of creation. He comes alive for us to in the celebrations of life, especially in their liturgical expression.

In times of great, even turbulent emotion, the word of God in the scriptures (for example in Psalm 139) brings its peaceful message. There is movement from an erroneous assumption that love, acceptance, security, success, closeness and even salvation itself depends on our ability to do the correct thing. God touches us where the spirit is divided from itself.

When we meet God in this way we are moved from self-absorption and pre-occupation with the negative in us. Our fear of abandonment by another or our shame or guilt causes us to deny or repress the real self. This can impel us to behave out of a lack of awareness. This puts the focus back on self and our limitations. We act out of addictions and compulsions. We bury things too unpleasant to face in our unconscious mind. Our poor self-esteem can then become an obstacle to our acceptance of the unconditional nature of the love of God.

Scripture is not a book of pious thoughts. It is the story of God and a people. But it is particularly a story of God and the response of individual people. The way we see it and interpret it writes the story of our lives. Our lives are scripted by the totality of our attitudes, formed from our earliest days by the experience of life. In consequence, we often repress the divine reality deep within us. It is underneath the emotional weeds that from childhood have tied us to limited images of God and religion. Secular culture often nourishes these weeds, intensifying human brokenness with all its consequences. Finding the true God who is hidden by the distractions of life is best achieved when we move from self-absorption towards the God of love.

Even the Bible itself in part has a limited view of God – interwoven with the loosely historical events which it interprets. Yet at the core of the Bible is a God of mercy that comes into full view first when Jesus comes. The life of Jesus is our best interpretation of the scriptures. Fundamentalism does a disservice to our search for the God of the scriptures, who searches for me as I am.

Our praying the Bible can sometimes hit the wrong key for us. If we pray 'the kingdom of God is at hand, repent and believe the good news', low self-esteem might impel us to focus on the word 'repent'. This could turn us in on ourselves. We might then fail to note the importance of belief in the nearness of the kingdom and the hope that it brings.

Our family of origin, our culture, can arrest our identity development. We might appear strong, competent, emotionally and spiritually healthy, while inside feel confused, lonely or lost. We overreact to things outside us and underreact to all that is hidden within. We invent self-defeating coping strategies, like a strong urge to control self and others or we take flight from intimacy or identify with rigid, dogmatic or authoritarian aspects of our culture. Perhaps this is a root cause of our addictions. If we are not to lapse into gambling, alcohol, drugs or other compulsions, we need to meet the real self within.

It is in this sense that Paul VI said that it is necessary to know humanity in order to know God. John Paul II says that Christ the redeemer reveals man to himself. Our journey to realising the divinity of Jesus is to accept his humanity. Somehow Jesus could not help caring, especially for the sinner and the wounded.

Space and silence for meeting Jesus change our focus. When we start with the person of Jesus we begin letting go into God. We set out on a spiritual journey that also brings human freedom. As we commit ourselves to this ongoing process, our unconscious becomes purified. The roots of guilt which say within, 'You did something wrong', and point to a terrifying God are torn up. Our image begins to change from an implacable God – as if from the punisher to my mother or from the policeman watching to my teacher. The shame which says, 'You are a mistake' starts being uprooted. The image of a tyrant God before whom we are powerless gives way to a God of Freedom who lifts us to safety from the barrenness of the desert where there is no hope.

When we know love and lose our fear of rejection, shame turns to self-esteem and guilt to awareness and recognition. We are set free for facing the truth, for reflective living and for positive thinking. We break out of our isolation to take risks in living real community. We become more committed to contact with the God who is accompanying us on the road to freedom. When our nature calls us back to our own self secure ways we will hear God still calling us out. His care is enough. The world of change no longer frightens. It is a world of variety, joy and inspiration. We are willing to reach out and touch our pilgrim companions. We tell them where to find bread. We can sub-stitute the beautiful and pleasurable for gloom and darkness.

Our thoughts, words, deeds and omissions can now be evaluated in the pure light of the gospel.

However, we must also choose. Our will is important. We must act out of the real world and the true God. A little humour is the sauce. We become owners of our own baggage rather than blame others. As owners we become actors rather than reactors. We are leaders. Thus our parish human development pro-grammes are a necessary foundation for the spiritual journey. Only in this way do we learn to co-operate rather than control, to heal rather than hurt, to be open rather than closed, to understand rather than blame, to include rather than exclude, to clarify rather than confuse – all of which are essential to effective leadership in social and spiritual development.

Yet, ultimately, for humans and for their community God is the starting-point. It is through our knowledge of him that we discover how much we need to be friendly to self and how that friendship is to be engendered. The interior civil war of acceptance or rejection is ended. When that war is raging we can't really reach out to others. It makes so much noise within that we can't even reach out to the God that loves us anyway. When we meet God we know that we can let every mistake become a joy too because it can be a learning experience.

In God, too, our love-inspired gaze finds him in everyone. We let God be God, the world be the world and people be people. Allowing ourselves to be who and what we are, our way of action moves towards love, our search for knowledge becomes insight and our prayer becomes worship.

Prayerfulness aligns us with the spirit within; this unity draws all things together. With this prayer at the heart of all that we do in parish life our pastoral activity cannot degenerate into boredom. We need the encouragement and support of each other to maintain our praying momentum. How often do we know where true nourishment is to be found and yet settle for easier more reachable substitutes? It is the strong sense of the people's faith that brings priests back to the core of their vocation.

We have a God of goodness to reveal the answer to every human problem. Come, good reader, join us in our search for him and his way. The Church is the means he offers, the vehicle for the pilgrim journey. Come on board for the trip to the wonders of life and love that will never end. The liturgy provides the special place for uniting our life with God's life. You are invited to come back to a renewed Church where you will find inner peace.

II
TOUCHES IN LITURGY

In a New Year message in 1980, our bishop, Peter Birch, gave thanks for a 'remarkable decade in the history of our diocese', when we 'were blessed with many blessings from God'. He spoke of a 'clear need for development of peace'. He said that there was 'so much for prayer to do', so that 'the good around would win through over all the evil around'. Peace and harmony can come, they will come if we all work for them 'in spirit and in truth'.

He called 'for real ecumenism' – the willingness to share our spiritual food and warmth with those who differ from us in religious practice. We must work for political peace – enough hard words have been said and heard; it is time now to extend the hand of friendship. 'We must work for peace in the north [of Ireland] – how does one value a life that is cut off in hate?'

'We must work for harmony between employers and workers – there is too much at stake in our country for sectional selfishness. We must work to see that country and town are not in conflict even when they differ. We must work for real unity and harmony among our young people and those in charge of them.'[2]

We see that prophetic invitation as equally valid today. Harmony comes through Christ. Liturgy is where we meet Jesus – in the people gathered, in the word, in the priest presiding, in the significance of sharing Christ's body and blood. It is where we are redeemed, changed for love by the experience of knowing Jesus. Our attempts at intelligent, full and active conscious participationbring us into touch with God and in his Spirit to help us know and love each other.[3] Our liturgy group works and reflects on how to create a Christ – centred community of love.

Sheila Coady of our liturgy group tells of our struggle to be active in her 'No People – No Liturgy' article in *The Colliery Christians*.[4] Our group came into existence as the parish underwent a renewal. During our mission each of us was challenged to reflect on our calling through baptism to serve and to take up our baptismal responsibilities by participating fully in the life of the local Church, the parish. In the words of Fr Enda Lyons, 'No one is called simply to be served by the Church, but rather that everyone in it is called to serve in it and be a partner in service.'[5]

In the parish we are very fortunate to be able to have so many opportunities to be 'partners in service' and to play an active role in the life and liturgy of the community. The celebration of the parish liturgy is one of the areas where everyone takes part in a personal special way. Vatican II in the *Constitution on the Sacred Liturgy* describes it as 'the summit' of Church life and also as a celebration of the life of the Church. 'The liturgy is thus the outstanding means by which the faithful can express in their lives and manifest to others the mystery of Christ and the real nature of the Church.'[6] Nowhere has 'the active participation of the faithful' been so clearly stated and worked out as in this document. We are all challenged to celebrate the liturgy in such a way that each of us is actively involved, not as spectators but as actors. If we are to take up our call to be actors and not spectators in celebrating the liturgy, we must get involved in the preparation and shaping as well as the celebrating. This means that our liturgy ought to be related to, and a celebration of the life of, the parish and all its members.

The liturgy is where Sheila and her colleagues provide a real opportunity for creating and celebrating community. It is the great weekly meeting of the people. We have only one mass in each Church on Saturday and Sunday to minimise fragment-ation. It is where we are most consciously Christ's people.

The late Bishop Birch often promoted 'Unity or Community in various forms.'[7] 'Unity is essential to Christianity', he wrote in what was to be his final pastoral to the Church in Ossory (Lent 1981). He went on to speak about the unity brought about by the mass from the penitential section to the sign of peace before communion.

We, like him, see 'sin and selfishness' as divisive causes of 'tension and tragedy', as the prayer of the mass put it one Sunday. At the beginning of mass we make good the advice of Jesus – if we have had a quarrel or a disagreement and we remember it as we are going to the altar, we should go back home and make it up and come back to the altar then, or at some other time. This is a striking way of putting it.

'A conscious move towards contrition, forgiveness and unity with our neighbour, as well as with God should then be a preparation for every mass. We should not miss it when we go to mass. Each time we attend should bring us closer to unity, and so we ought not lightly skip that part of the liturgy which is designed to ease us into the state where we can come closer to God and to one another by publicly renouncing our sins and failures and we should try to mean it. When we say it we confess both to God and to our brothers and sisters. We renew this desire for unity later on in mass by the sign of peace before communion.

'We must be aware of sin in the community around us and we are part of that community. We may be guilty of sin here. Let me say a word about community, because mass and sacraments are community actions. They make community. There is a lot of talk about community just now and it is possible people will be put off by constant reference to it. A community of people is something that grows, one part linked to another. Its growth can be quick or slow or even killed, so if people shut themselves off at mass, at the sacraments they are preventing community forming. Selfishness kills. Our liturgy is our expression of who we are, where we have come from and where we are going. Sharing the bread in our desire to be eucharist for another so that "all may be one".'

Both in the human and spiritual sense we are social beings. We depend upon help from each other. The temptation to settle down with the healing growth spoken of in the previous section is a seduction. If we really come to Jesus we will soon be sent by him ... Having bound up our broken self-image he will be sending us to help others discover their value in his sight. With his healing for our wounded hearts we will feel his Spirit send us to heal the cleavage between love and sexuality in this permissive age.

Knowing that we are loved by him and that he loved us first, we feel more capable of giving love in return with our words, attitudes and actions. Without a sense of Church-community animated with the presence of Christ, it is too difficult to see signs of hope, to pass beyond the emotional to discover truth itself.

When we are in touch with reality, reflected in the flesh and blood of Jesus, in the prophets and the mystics, the clearer the view we have of what is now happening. Then the more exact too will be our picture of what is about to happen. We can read the signs of the times. The breadth, width, height and depth of the Church correctly understood provides the richest context for our human pilgrimage towards fulfilment of life and love.

Our attempts to celebrate life in the sacred space of liturgical memorial, points towards an axis for all pastoral planning. Are we not really sent to tell of him whom we have met in word and sacrament? Those whom we then invite to 'come and see' ... will themselves be sent with the same mission.

III
CELEBRATES LIFE

Appreciation is often expressed for our invitation to involvement – particularly in the liturgy at funerals. The extent to
which liturgies celebrate the life of the deceased is much
appreciated. People feel a presence that brings consolation and
even a sense of joy. The integration of the person's life into the
mass of burial through symbols at the offertory procession,
celebrates both human and divine love. What is heard and
understood is the continuity of the life of the baptised. The hope
that it brings alleviates the pain of the moment. The unity of
prayer and singing creates a communion of sharing that is
personal and spiritual. The presence of the alienated or the
lapsed makes it special too. The integration of intercession,
memorial and a message of hope opens hearts to a new
awakening of the spirit.

Nobody (except the occasional cleric!) objects to the forty-
five minutes we spend commending our departed ones to God.
In the old days it would be described as a high mass. Now it is
one of the most significant parts of our Christian pilgrimage.

There are many opportunities for becoming involved in
bringing our parish life to our liturgical celebrations. People
get involved as ministers of the eucharist, members of the choir,
readers of the word, participants in the offertory procession and
the prayers of the faithful. They help with caring for the Church
and with collections and of course in planning and preparing
our various celebrations. It is the mission or task of the liturgy
group to facilitate everyone in praying, singing and engaging
with the celebration.

At the liturgy groups inception the parish was preparing
to celebrate first holy communion and confirmation. It was
decided to highlight the significance of these two major steps
in the Christian journey by inviting families of all the children
involved to participate in the introduction, penitential rite and
our offertory procession of the mass and in the prayers of the

faithful. This is now an accepted part of our preparation for the sacraments.

Sometimes we have extravagant liturgies. On St Patrick's Eve 1991 we came together, first in the Church and later at a social function to celebrate all forms of involvement in parish life. The celebration began as the children danced to *céilí* music right up to the altar and dressed it for mass.

'The Lord is Present,' sang the combined choirs in the words of the folk hymn for the solemn liturgical entrance. The mass, celebrating the first anniversary of our mission and the involvement of the people in the life of the parish had got underway in an atmosphere of excitement, friendship and unity. In seven separate processions to the altar, the involvement of people in living the faith brought by St Patrick was recalled.

We touched into our Celtic spirituality with the shamrock and the flowers, the hospitality and the care and the instruments of mirth and joy. The shamrock was blessed. We introduced a new family, come to live among us, and had a welcoming ceremony for the youngest Christian as the water, from the well of St Patrick, was blessed and sprinkled. We had gone back to our common Christian origins, St Patrick being our parish as well as our national patron. We repented anew of our sins, selfishness and divisions. Then the school community brought the white shawl, oil and light of the newly baptised consecrated to be the light of Christ and clothed with a new Christian dignity. The parents, priests and teachers in community clothe us in Christ as channels of the Spirit. At each of the three movements of anointing, clothing and letting the light shine, we confessed our failures to the string of a folk *Kyrie*.

After glory, praise and thanksgiving, and the opening prayer of the mass – the dignity of Christ in his word was acclaimed. The fourth procession introduced the readers of the word, and those who serve the word through prayer and ministry. We opened our hearts to the proclamation of the first reading. The choir led everyone in the psalm, 'Be with me,

Lord, when I'm in trouble'.

The second reading was our call to be a 'light to the nations'. We welcomed to the sanctuary representatives of the migrants and the missionary, the sisters, members of the St Vincent de Paul Society, the Legion of Mary and those involved in the missionary trust of the Church.

As we stood for the gospel, we heard of the seventy-two disciples sent out two by two. We began to understand why we had seventy-two participants (excluding the clergy, the choirs and the altar servers) in this mass. The seven processions symbolised a united people. All the participants on the night represented the thirty-six parish groups, organisations and services that prepare the way for Christ, to bring his peace into our hearts and homes.

After the Gospel, a representative of our interdenominational community council introduced avenues of peace through community enterprise, a variety of youth work, education and shared pilgrimage, as we opened our hearts to the call of our Churches for peace on this St Patrick's Day.

Dr Robert McCarthy, our local Church of Ireland rector, touched everyone as he underlined the many messages of St Patrick, both for a way of being community and in the path towards peace. The offertory procession, brought the groups who promote prayer and retreats, those who link the eucharist with the housebound and those intimately associated with the soul of the Church. As the incense rose around the altar and the *Pobal Dé* and the offertory gifts, the Taize 'O Christe Jesu' lifted us all to await the special moment of consecration. The Celtic 'Christ be beside Me', the folk 'Here I Am' and the popular song of 'Father, Son and Spirit' accompanied the huge congregation to holy communion.

The eucharist was solemnly brought to the sick in our community, as is done on Holy Thursday. Many of our forty eucharistic ministers bring communion to the sick each Sunday. As we left this mass of unity and peace, so splendidly organised by our liturgy group, the crowds were joyously singing 'Walk

in the Light'. Every heart was touched by the continuing relevance of the good news proclaimed by St Patrick.

On the feast of Christ the King, the last day of the Church's
year, we celebrate and call to mind the entire life of our parish
by gathering together representatives of all the various groups
in a special entrance procession to our eucharist. Traditionally,
the month of November is the time of year when we remember
in a special way all those whom we loved and who are no
longer with us. This is a high point in people's devotional life
when all write their own loved ones' names in a Book of Life
for our November offertory masses. A special mass where all
those bereaved during the year take part is especially appreciated. The liturgy group prepares a special procession of light
for the mass to remind us of the hope and the triumph of
Christ's resurrection over the darkness of sorrow and death.
We reflectively journey through our pain and let go into
Christ's love those whom we hunger to touch once more.

In Advent, a time of joyful anticipation and preparation for
the birth of Christ, we try to learn something from how the
ancestors of Jesus prepared for his coming. We made a Jesse
tree. For each of the four Sundays of Advent a number of
symbols representing the spiritual ancestors of Jesus are
brought forward during the offertory procession and placed
on this family tree of Jesus. Together with all the general
preparations for the Christmas liturgies, a special emphasis is
placed on remembering our emigrants during the Christmas
masses. From then until Pentecost participation continues in
family and community events.

When we reconvene after summer we are blessed with very
stimulating workshops. The liturgy group sees its task as
keeping in tune with the Church's liturgical calendar. It
therefore highlights the significant feast days and festivals.
Material provided by the Ossory diocesan liturgy committee
has been most helpful in providing a meaningful liturgy for
Holy Week. The parish committee appreciates such help. They
also find that *Intercom* is a rich liturgical resource. The parish

bulletin eventually chosen to be most appropriate provides the scripture readings for the Sunday mass together with an explanation of the gospel with its relevant holy communion reflection. However, our most creative resource is Fr Willie Purcell, the assistant priest in Clogh. His involvement with the Liturgy Institute in Carlow, his chairmanship also of the Irish Church Music Association and his subsequent involvement with the Irish Episcopal Commission for the Liturgy, keeps him and us in touch with an abundance of rich resources. On our parish team Willie is the parish priest for liturgy. His musical genius and ability with youth keep our Church young at heart.

IV
RENEWS THE HEART

A Church of celebration and joy, even in the face of life's traumas and absurdities, is young at heart. Nobody, least of all the young, rejects love, joy, peace, patience, kindness, goodness, faithfulness, gentleness and self-control (Gal. 5). Anybody who lives by the spirit or walks in the spirit of wisdom, understanding, counsel, fortitude, knowledge and godliness (Isa. 12) finds open doors. A Church, that is forever young and living the 'gifts of the Spirit' will always be in touch.

An appearance of wealth and power, an apparently legalistic approach to human situations, (as for example, in marriage laws) a preoccupation with financial matters and buildings – all tend to reinforce an institutional image of the Church. For many young people and some adults too this is the only Church there is. How do we bridge the gap for those who seek Christ but instead find only the institution? It is so difficult to accept that our personal attitudes, our difficulties in grasping the significance and implications of renewal, and many of our pastoral methods hinder rather than help us to make real human contact?

Many years ago Paul VI asked us to meditate on the concept

of reform.[8] 'We may recognise that all too often we priests are the most sceptical of all as to the possibility of modifying customs and temperaments, of renewing souls,' he said. 'Perhaps,' he continued, 'this is due to our greater experience of human weakness, to a sense of defeat with respect to the ideal that on the day of our ordination we believed we could reach. We dreamed. Then we were enthusiastic. We planned heroic programmes – we prayed so much then ... And now we find ourselves commonplace, mediocre, cautious, almost insensitive. After so many years of the priesthood we perhaps see ourselves less good and loving and lordless, less capable of prayer, of humility and strength, than we were in the first days of our ministry.'

He went on to say, 'We must make our hearts young again. We must discover a new enthusiasm and strength. Why? Because we really believe that the Holy Spirit can infuse new life and keep us young at heart. We really believe that divine forces move us. We believe that the Lord helps our efforts. "We are God's helpers", says St Paul. Therefore, if we believe this, if we believe in this reality that Christ has brought to the world, in the energy grace imparts to us in our wretchedness, then we believe that we can be young, happy and energetic again. We can renew our poor tired spirit,' said that reforming Pope. He went on to say: 'If we are sceptical, then unconsciously we have sinned against faith; we have succumbed to an erroneous notion of practical success. It drowns out our spiritual yearnings.

'We believe that in us, in addition to the son of Adam, there is the Son of God, who has come to graft into this poor humanity new energies, and for him who accepts them these energies are powerful.'

Pope Paul VI's dictum that we can do more by loving than by knowing, that we must be concerned more with love than clarity of ideas is important. But at the same time we need some structure to focus our collective attention, facilities and services on the real needs of people so that we can devise means of making a more effective pastoral impact.

Many priests admit dissatisfaction, concern and helplessness. We sense an inability to help people to a religion which they quest – a religion of joy which speaks to them. When confronted with a demand for an intensely personal faith, or because we realise that people may find liturgy meaningless we cry out, 'What more can we do?'

Renewing the heart is not the priest's responsibility alone. The whole Christian community plays a part. The influence of parents, teachers and parish workers must not be minimised. 'Example is more efficacious than precept,' a seminary colleague often repeated. But our example cannot always match expectations. Neither does our concern for others and the gospel values (1 Cor. 13: 4-6) which they demand of Christians. 'Churchianity out; Christianity in': 'Catholic but not Christian'; 'Hypocrites' are familiar slogans.

To be young at heart perhaps we need to be attentive to the needs of the young. Can we see them in the context of the traditional formative influences and at the same time try to meet new dominant influences in their growth? The young need very personal support until they are capable of consistently making mature and independent decisions. This is true also of our Church. People are growing to commitment in a mature and independent way and are more at ease with complexity.

God does not want us to walk blindly. He does not want us to fragment into 'social, political or ideological pulls' with eventual tensions and breakaways. Yet where we accept individuality, a variety of riches and different perspectives, disagreement is inevitable. It is part of our teasing-out of our many experiences. It is an aspect of learning. Why then do we fear disagreement so much, particularly with those in authority? I think it has much to do with the fact that often we experience such disagreement as victims rather than learners. Adults as well as youth, the leader as well as the led, must be aware of all the dominant influences in our life. Otherwise we walk leaderless, in confusion. We experience a sense of loss, live in ritual deadness or by mere adherence to rules.

This is not the will of God. Where everyone accepts that God alone can really cause a community to grow into a caring Christian one, the breath of His Spirit breathes anew into our dry bones (Zech. 37).

The spirit, being the soul of the Church, will keep us close to its heart. All Church institutions or legal statutes that are appropriate only for the adolescent stage of religious growth need development, renewal or abandonment. Our more modern mentality calls for a greater freedom from the mere experience of authority so that the authority of experience will be able to guide collaborative decisions of the whole people of God. The Spirit calls us

> to act justly,
> to love tenderly,
> to walk humbly with God,
> always to be open to youthful dreams.

Perhaps this is something more of the heart than of the conscience. How often we meet people who regard the informed conscience in much the same light as they do disagreement with authority. It too is experienced as oppressive. On the other hand, the heart is acceptable as the symbolic centre of our attitudes and emotions towards others and the organ which sustains the life of the whole body. St Bernard of Clairvaux is reputed to be the one who used it also as a symbol of our attitude to God. An appreciation of Jesus as a man of the heart led to exploration of the meaning of the heart in scripture. In scripture it always refers to the intelligent heart, the good conscience in action.

As the incarnation of the love of God, the heart of the man Jesus became the symbol of unity of his inner life. His heart pierced on the cross is the heart of God, wounded out of love for us. This simple symbol, the pierced heart, is the focal point of the fourth gospel, the hour when Jesus was exalted. Jesus's life led to that hour. For St John it too was the moment when

Jesus was lifted up on the cross into the glory of God. This is the hour of the triumph of love as we profess it. God is love.

For people in general the heart – even the pierced heart for those who love, is seen as unitive and life-giving. Love is *the* reason for living. Ultimately the love in God's heart is the only one that cannot be broken or diminished by circumstances. The welfare of humanity is secured by the extent that our hearts are strengthened by the heart of God.

It was from this pierced heart that the Church was born. If it is to be forever young the primacy of the heart as understood by the mystics, poets and creative artists needs to be more firmly established. The great renewal movements in Church history were mostly youth-inspired: all the movers were young, idealistic and adventurous. This is the time for shaping the Church through the perspective of the young. They will put a renewed heart in it.

V

FOR A CHURCH EVER YOUNG

If youth are not drawn into our parish life we cease to be a living community alive with the newness of the Spirit. While all age groups are important special energies are needed to keep the ancient faith relevant to the newest members. This is *the* priority of our parish, for our young priest, the youth and many of their parents. It helps keep the rest of us alive, consistently calling the whole parish back to the Irish bishops' *Challenge in the Young Church* (Chapter 1, Section 3).

The noblest call of the heart is to see another as divine. There is inspiration to do anything for the beloved. Beyond the emotional level the opportunity to give of oneself in service to others is everybody's right and need. Some difficulty arises in providing opportunities which are appropriate to the person giving. There is obviously much generosity in the young. Equally obvious is that the ways in which this can be expressed are restricted by the fact that their resources and skills are limited. We devise situations in which young people are challenged to give of themselves but these are rarely exploited. A short intensive commitment is more suitable to the young than a long-term project. It is extraordinary how little young people have been exposed to the needs of others around them. The problem here is largely one of organisation and communication.

Our youth service aims to get young people to focus on some local community need and *under guidance* do something definite about it. What is important here is that any such project should provide an opportunity for growth for the participants. This calls for proper preparation. Youth ministry is only one of our many agencies involved with young people. It is only one of the factors affecting their growth and development.

To be accepted and understood by others is very important to young people. Genuine appreciation of what they are means an acceptance of their dignity as persons. Low self-esteem cripples the creativity of too many young people. They are deeply conscious of their own inadequacies and this can result in a deep feeling of insecurity, intensifying their low self-esteem.

A key figure in providing acceptance and reassurance is likely to be an understanding adult. This may be a parent or teacher – religious or priest. Often what is needed is a person in a less clear-cut authority position who can act as a confidant. To maintain and make permanent what has been accomplished by our young priest, leaders are being trained with the assistance of the Ossory youth services.

Contrary to popular belief young people often live their lives within a very narrow range of experience, much of it dull and boring. This in turn finds expression in anti-social behaviour. This arises from escapist entertainment or 'drifting' along. It is true that for many young people an expected curiosity and sense of adventure have been replaced by apathy and timidity. Consumerism is making the problem more difficult. Fear, anxiety, low self-esteem and deviant tendencies in some are the consequence of an over-burdened lifestyle. Some have no real escape. Their inability to trust and their pseudo-maturity predisposes them to learn their social skills from the most undesirable aspects of the pop and media culture. Increase in anti-social behaviour, even actual crime, is inevitable and small rural communities are not immune. Challenging those wider issues has proved impossible. We have been ignored in our attempts by all levels of justice, health and community care agencies.

So we have tried to tap into the sense of adventure, curiosity about life and hunger for new experience that are still character-istic of the young. They are the most valuable assets they have in facing the problem of shaping their lives. We see it as our task to encourage such assets. We do this also in the area of their religious formation. The Church's message is relevant today only if it strikes people as such. The Church in its official liturgy and rules speaks a language which doesn't reach them. This argues for a presence to young people which is seen as concerned, personal and exciting. The way to the mind of many a young person is through the heart.

A characteristic of today's youth culture is the quest for freedom. They respond when encouraged to take control of their own lives. Our youth ministry group, folk choirs and youth clubs try to provide opportunities for participation, reflection and freedom. There is no manipulation. A genuine community-based youth service is a key to their freedom. They too are entitled to speak for themselves. Youth ministry pro-vides gospel-inspired criteria.

During adolescence the influence of friends is a very significant factor in a young person's development. It may conflict with the influences of school or group or home. The effect of our youth ministry group and the youth club has been a leaven, involving many young people and revealing to them their own extraordinary talents. The musical, sports and drama groups brought pride in achievement and acquired skill. A youth training programme on a residential weekend has brought a willingness to learn new skills for personal and social development. Discos, youth camps, hostelling and foreign travel has widened the range of experience. Learning by doing reverses the downward spiral of self-esteem.

The Church has always had a service interest in education. In this area evangelisation is by no means our only interest. We take steps to equip the individual with the skills and tools of living in a modern society. We encourage participation in self-development, in community and in living the faith. In particular we see the need to help young people cultivate mature relationships as this is of special importance for their well-being and as a preparation for marriage.

'The best kind of preparation for the young does not need to mention marriage. It is more important to train young people in personal relationships with boys, girls, adults, than have formal teaching. This is important if, later, a boy-girl relationship is to grow into a permanent loving commitment. Our natural reaction to boy-girl relationships was one of mistrust and suspicion, whereas trust and encouragement could foster their every opportunity to show that their growing relationship fits in with their understanding of God and especially that God is love. Opportunities for helping young people occur in schools and through youth clubs' (Ossory priests at their pastoral conference, 1977).[9] The quality of relationships also effect areas like delinquency, drink, attitudes to sexual mores and authority figures.

True love is learned. Relationships can be both bad and good. Skill is required to enable young people to develop all their personal resources. Youth workers must know about and possess such skill. Learning these skills demands an ability to see what the young person needs, rather than wants. It is in this context that the young discover and appreciate the relevance of religion to daily living.

Much is made by adults too of their need for freedom. A key aspect of freedom is responsibility. We recognise that one of the important tasks in life is to assume responsibility for our own lives. We share this with young people in small things initially. Total freedom brings fear and loneliness. There has to be gradual sharing for growth. It is the same with adults beginning to assume their rightful place in the life of the Church. Cultivating positive relationships is a task of leadership. To assume new responsibility calls for the practice of the skills required together with formation and ongoing renewal. Our young are not only the Church of tomorrow but the Church of today.

For the young Church to be solidly rooted it must be aware of its journey through culture, prejudices and traditions. The perspective of the young is that of observed truth. The vision Churchmen have is that of revealed truth. When it comes to what actually happens in our lives, as distinct from what we would like to happen, the observed reality is life as we live it. We are trying to come to revealed truth by way of the human reality and how God is present in it. Only thus can we cope with alternative pulls. It is God who helps us to go against the flow in choosing the good in our culture and traditions and accepting the primacy of decision over feeling.

---

1   Eucharistic Prayer 4. Cf P Collins CM (All Hallows College, Dublin), *Intimacy and the Hungers of the Human Heart* (1991); *Growing in Health and Grace*, (1991). Cf. T Keating OSCO (Founder of the Centering Prayer Movement and Contemplative Outreach, Spencer, Mass.) *Open Mind, Open Heart; Finding Grace at the Centre; The Heart of the World; And the World Made Flesh*. His tapes from Seton Hall, New Jersey Institute are excellent.

2   From my personal file of his letters, messages and community radio interviews.

3   Conciliar decree on the bishop's pastoral office in the church. *The Diocesan Clergy* (Sect. 30); Constitution on the Sacred Liturgy (Pt 4, Sect. 14).

4   Clogh Parish Pastoral Team, *The Colliery Christians*, Clogh Parish Pastoral Council (1992).

5   E Lyons, *Partnership in Parish*, The Columba Press (1987).

6   *Constitution on the Sacred Liturgy* (Sect 2). See also *On the Nature of the Sacred Liturgy* (Ch. 1, Sect 5–12).

7   See note 2 *supra*.

8   Paul VI, *Osservatore Romano* (from a personal file of clippings).

9   From my personal file. The conference was an exciting experience of
     collaboration from neighbourhood house meetings on seven major human
     themes through parish reports listened to by diocesan services involving
     priests, religious and laity, young and old working together to bring the
     fruits of the council to systemic fruition.

CHAPTER 5

LIFE AS WE LIVE IT

I
THROUGH OUR CULTURE AND TRADITIONS

When the current team of clergy arrived in this parish in 1989, involving the laity in the mission of the Church was a central aspect of pastoral policy. Accepting the traditions and culture of the parish and its effect on people's lives gave a radical focus to our mission. The question of justice and a sense of being treated unjustly in the past deeply influenced pastoral concerns. In accepting life as it is lived in Clogh the place of people in the Church raised issues of a social nature. The burning issues seemed to revolve around justice.

Each year we looked at one of these issues. It was in this context that we examined the place of women in the Church in our second year. At a symposium, Sr Stanislaus Kennedy gave an inspirational place to the 'Women in the Modern Church'. The women took the lead in the liturgies, including the application of the gospel to motherhood, mission, mystic, and ministry during Lent. At a public meeting the missionaries met the women of the parish. There was also an evening on justice during the parish mission.

Our preparation drew attention to the Irish bishops' commitment to the equality of men and women at the meeting in June 1990.[1] 'Women rank equally with men,' they said. Our parish explored where our practice did not match this teaching.

The parish pastoral council accepted the recommendations for change necessary in our parish. We tried to put in place a ministry of service to need in place of any form of superiority and power being exercised over others in the parish. Wherever in the institutional priorities, there was denial of the 'equality of dignity' we provided alternative strategies.

The parish began to cherish in particular the woman as preacher of the gospel, as servant of the community, as mother and Christian. The Irish bishops stressed the equality of men and women and their equal dignity. They asserted that ordained ministry 'is not a form of superiority over others'. They went on to admit that 'the discussion of the question of the ordination of women clearly reveals that many people see the priesthood as a form of superiority and power'.

Priesthood as a form of superiority and power is deeply ingrained in the culture of our community. In the 1930s the question of dignity and justice for the coalminers got lost in an ideological conflict. The needs of these faith-filled workers and their union's struggle on their behalf led to their excommunication from the Church. The circumstances leading to this conflict with its consequent alienation is inexplicable to the mentality of the post-Vatican II Church. Human misery and very poor working and living conditions had to take the last place because of fear of Communism. Some of the ethos of that time may be gathered from Appendix 1. It tries to indicate how a policy dictated by an ideological fear can hurt and bruise. Excommunication of faith-filled fathers and brothers was a cause of alienation and hurt. The emergence of the buried pain and anger from that time with its subsequent influence on their attitude to the Church had a major impact on laity involvement.

Those caught in this conflict between loyalty to the struggle for justice and fidelity to their Church are now passing on to God. The tears, pain and alienation of many a home are only now percolating into the consciousness of the parish as Church. Our diamond jubilee celebrations for the Church built with the help of miners' donations, directly debited weekly from their inadequate wages sought – symbolically and sacramentally – forgiveness and reconciliation. Central to the celebrations were the prayers for healing and forgiveness for a Church of power and superiority. All those excommunicated had been reconciled with the Church. The Church now sought reconciliation with the people. It was the most profoundly prayerful and peaceful moment ever experienced by all those present at the celebration. It was the morning for general absolution. It was the day the women remembered their mothers' pain, giving thanks for a freer Ireland and a renewed Church, and for equality of dignity.

This experience led us to the theme of our third year. Our energies were directed to the marginalised. Our concern for the unemployed, the migrant and the job-seeker, led to development programmes with ecumenical and inter-parish initiatives. *The Colliery Christians* produced by Clogh Parish Team graphs it growth and development.[2]

Other issues tackled included the provision of permanent leadership for youth. A pastoral letter to parents with suggestions for coping with the new teen culture was prepared by the three members of the clergy in interdenominational unity. Coping with the secular media culture was seen as an urgent need. Applying the gospel, in its liturgical season, to the traumas of life was the function of all our ecumenical pastorals. (See Christmas message, Appendix 5).

There is an outreach to the most marginalised – those affected by broken relationships, addictions and poverty. The St Vincent de Paul shop linked our poor in helping to educate the poor of Pakistan. Their 'Till Your Own Garden' scheme, the FÁS course and social employment scheme aimed to restore pride in creativity and self reliance. Our Heritage Weekend in September 1993 created an awareness of the rich heritage of our parish and of the existence of much skill to cope with the demands of the present. It showed too the financial potential of God's gift of nature to refresh visitors, seeking a renewal of body and spirit. The Church was brought to the people by area masses, particularly in housing schemes and in a neighbourhood Advent programme.

There is a sense that this 'Work of Justice' is just beginning.

For the one that says it is sixty years too late, there are ten who say that it is great that the people are becoming the Church.

Yet there is a darker side which is a concern to us all. People gather for different kinds of reasons. Sometimes they search for comfort, using drink or drugs or occasionally the occult. People sometimes use other people this way too. Young people can be led astray not only by the use of addictive drugs in the material sense but by other people using them in such a way.

It is particularly sad when older people act as a scandal to the little ones. It is difficult to reach out to people living in the shadows, prisoners of past alienation, who refuse to be touched by the way of Christ. On the one hand as a Christian community we all have a strong wish that nobody feel rejected or beyond the eternal love of God. On the other hand forms of behaviour which lead people away from respect for love and the dignity of the person and the sensitivity of the human relationship must be rejected. How do we reject the darkness and at the same time show the care and love that Christ has for all people? If pain, darkness, even evil are corrupting a community, then what can be done about it? We realise that this is a problem in modern Ireland. There are many good things about our world. The care and commitment of so many of our families, the involvement of people in maintaining community life and the life of the Church are a cause of great joy. The fear is that if we do not recognise and heal the sickness that it may become incurable and infectious. A bad apple corrupts the good around it.

We feel helpless as a parish particularly when we see children suffer. The state's contribution is entirely negative except for the excellence of its educational policies. We have an obligation to protect the young and help them grow in friendship and trust, hope and happiness, joy and celebration. We need to be aware of the darkness. The fact that the light of people's goodness is stronger than any darkness fills us with Christian hope.

However, there is a need for enough people to recognise that darkness begins with a trickle but may increase to torrents of despair and disaster. When we as a community face up to the reality of the darkness around us then together we can journey into the light of hope. It takes courage to face reality which will not change unless we learn to accept the challenge to cope with its many expressions and aspects. Perhaps even the future of our young depends on how in the present we cope with this darkness. Justice demands it but we wait and pray to be shown how. We are listening – lest history is repeated. Global condemnation from a narrow perspective does more harm than good. How can we love enough? To let go of the past in honesty and truth is to live in the present in justice and love. For those who have the privilege of making all the decisions, the time has come to share the process with those who have to endure the consequences. We too are creators of culture but we will establish good traditions only if we share the decisions. Together we must name each other's gifts and put them at the service of our fellows.

II
CLAIMING OUR GIFTS FROM HIS SPIRIT

We have set free a hidden desire for genuine involvement in the Church and the people of the parish now test our willingness to facilitate real participation. Their history has taught them to distrust every form of authority. When they share in selecting those with the task of leadership they trust that their opinions will be respected. Resentment will follow if outsiders make all the decisions. Mere token involvement leads to anger. We all feel excluded – unless our anger is expressed assertively.

The openness of the people when allowed real participation helped me to explore my own attitude to the exercise of authority. We are all human. Priests, like other mortals, tend to shut down when ignored, rejected or if we sense a potential conflict.[3] We withdraw, pretend there is nothing wrong, go home and forget, go silent, welcome any distraction. At meetings where all the real decisions are made elsewhere the feeling uppermost in our minds is to quit attending. As a consequence meetings need to have as their primary objective the facilitation of two-way communication. Leadership is necessary to engage us in a process of dialogue and decision-making. For our part we often bring a wrong attitude to crucial meetings. This can be an obstacle when we need to hear the honest reaction of the laity.

Much of today's public comment and attitudes towards authoritarian institutions indicate anger – either passive or aggressive. Productive meetings at parish level are a necessity if such alienation is not to become permanent.

There is need for some basic agreement about objectives and function. We need to review our actions sensitive to each others experiences, particularly with regard to the work of the spirit. The only successful avoidance of such anger and alienation is the sense of our right to express what we feel and think. This is reinforced when we sense a positive response.

Preoccupation with the institution and its needs has to be balanced by the needs of the people of God. How these are most effectively to be ministered to is best discovered by parish visitation assisted by surveys of reactions to parish pastoral policy. The visit needs to have a specific purpose to raise it above the level of a social call (See Appendix 3). People who have had a significant experience are encouraged to minister to those with similar problems, for example, the bereaved, separated, widowed with family.

Providing the leadership that draws together the various charisms in the parish can be difficult. We need to be realistic about what we can do and from whom leadership is acceptable. We must know, value and enjoy our own special gift. We need to involve the maximum possible number in offering their skill or gift if we are to create a real genuine community. The newly converted, those who had a religious experience, sometimes give the credit to the group method. With formation their contribution to the prayer/scripture/faith aspects of parish life can be enormous.

Every community development phase needs to be in some way self-sufficient and self-perpetuating. If the priest is changed to another parish those remaining should be capable of maintaining the momentum. It is for this reason that we are building up our parish leadership team. We meet at least once each week except during holiday time. They share our vision and help clarify the function and objectives of the other groups.

Their help gives the priest space for spiritual and personal needs. The members appreciate our need of time for prayer, reflection, silence study, renewal. A huge amount of time goes into keeping abreast of Church teaching, research and preparation for our pastoral work. Areas demanding daily prayerful reflection in different skills and much preparation include:

- Worship – mass, sacraments, devotions, prayer groups
- Proclaiming the word – preaching, teaching, adult education, publicising, and evaluating
- Caring – counselling, meeting human needs in bereavement, sickness, pain, rejection, weakness, deprivation, boredom, strained relations, in listening to those angry and hurt by the Church
- Working with groups (which need constantly to be motivated) – development, enabling, spotting skills, building talents, creating space for gifts, finding and informing guest speakers
- Administration – organisation, co-ordination, finance, accountability, assessment, planning, building up, affirming, all with special difficulties.

All the parishes where I ministered were blessed with a wonderful spirit of community care. Natural leaders took excellent community initiatives. There were first-class schools, clubs and organisations. They were characterised by exemplary neighbourliness, strong faith, a rich devotional prayer life and a sense of cultural and religious heritage. Spot-lighting this in individuals often arouses that Irish demon – envy. Many enjoy bringing others 'down a peg or two'. Saintly, caring, untiring, promoters of goodness and truth, personifying all that is best in traditional Catholicism, may not necessarily be effective community builders, unless they have some skill in leadership.

It is for this reason that membership of the parish team was initially confidential. Though they work with us – sometimes almost on a voluntary full-time basis in the five areas mentioned – they prefer to do it quietly. It is a characteristic of rural communities that everybody desires to know what anybody knows. Yet the principle of confidentiality is increasingly accepted especially by those who have experience of its need in groups on which they have already served, for example, the school board, the Credit Union, the St Vincent de Paul conference.

Other ways in which the team offers help cannot strictly be called parish work. They free us to be pastorally with our own family, relations and friends in their time of need or to work within diocesan structures, organisations and charities. We have used the team's experience to work across divides with other Churches, in dialogue with the world on international issues and Third World poverty. They help us in creating awareness of injustice, coping with secularism, materialism, consumerism, permissiveness. They encourage us to maintain space and freedom for initiatives locally in the face of a new centralisation of authority within the Church. They encourage us too in taking time out for personal needs, recreational and spiritual.

The team members manifest a real spirit of service. They are caring, honest and open. They are willing to learn. They understand that if people have a real say in decisions which are taken, they are then more likely to help with implementation. Participation involves not only allowing people have a say but in taking that into account when the decision is being made. The team often remind us of what we have not heard. Traditionally lay people are intimidated by the articulate priest or religious. The contribution of the team in helping others to evaluate such articulate opinions in the context of agreed policy is essential if personal opinion is to lead to group consensus.

People want to be freed to be themselves and to work from the knowledge of their own strength. But someone must spur them on, motivate them and get the 'why' of the service purified. Ongoing conversion is always necessary for team members to enable each of us to do things for the right reasons.

We are allowed to serve Christ. Otherwise we manipulate. People giving service need to be formed in skills but also in a deepening of their faith and in the love which unifies everything. Efficiency and skill on their own do not build community. Prayer is essential – the Holy Spirit is *the* community leader.

Sensitivity to spiritual events and the spiritual meaning for us in human events grows largely from loving relationships. Spiritual intimacy with personal friends comes from the God they reveal – the one who loves me as I am. That is the God we on the team desire to reveal to each other and to every parishioner.

More and more people, even those who have a deep spiritual life, do not see the Church as a community to which they belong.[4] Some even experience the Church as an obstacle to their personal growth, spiritual and human. Most people see very little real connection between the natural talented community of their life and what they regard as the Church.

Many of the values of a community based on the gospel already exist in the basic daily relationships of much of Irish life. This is true even between the different Christian Churches as we saw in Chapter 3, Section 2. However, good pastoral practice calls for a strategy to create bonds of unity. The God that is made flesh in our own personal lives has a strong influence on people's ability to hear the gospel.

III
CREATING BONDS FOR UNITY

The Church is living through a radical transition. The response of people to change and new ideas varies from uncritical acceptance through critical and open consideration of all that is happening to unthinking rejection of all that is new. Many of our parishioners are full of new hope because they believe that a new age has dawned. Some are full of foreboding. Some are confused and others are lost. All face new difficulties. Our Church of tomorrow will grow out of the consensus of our people holding all these positions. Whatever our own personal views may be our job in part is to facilitate and participate in creating that consensus.

Our parish council members were greatly encouraged by their attendance at a seminar in Dublin on collaboration. There they saw that the NCPI believes that clergy and laity are equal in dignity and should work hand in hand. Priests and people must relate to each other in a more adult way. The feeling among the representative body for priests is that the clergy should let go of the control of the people. They believe that the task of the Church is so to empower lay people that their voice will be heard and that lay people's wisdom will be part of the Church. They admit that the more the Church tries to control people's lives the less authority it has. Imposing ways of living and acting is no longer acceptable, they concede. This seminar was helpful in finding a better way.

Most priests understand that the more people are given dictation from above the more the authority of Church leadership is undermined. Many committed people seem to think that they do not matter to the Church and feel no sense of belonging to it. They express feelings of frustration and regret about many aspects of Church life. They believe the Church is too authoritarian and not committed enough in practice to giving the laity a greater say in the life of the Church.

The overall impression received from that gathering was

that the people are lovingly concerned for the Church. All insist that it is important for people to be given an active role before they opt out. Our experience on the ground confirms that view. People want to respond. Each has a skill and way, but finds it hard to get into the system.

Since all are on a spiritual pilgrimage different levels of involvement are respected. The father in a family may do a splendid job without being in any group. There is a danger of elitism. So outreach is now a core consideration of our pastoral council. We empower people as a leaven for the whole community, consciously striving to avoid becoming a ghetto of cronies. To be the community's voice we are constantly listening. We respond to the call of parents, families, the poor and unemployed.

Parish visitation is a form of hearing. It is also a process of healing for the alienated whom we visit. They are invited to belong. Their help in evaluation is sought. Lay people become aware of their own values, strengths, and skills by being heard. Their involvement moves the parish towards accepting people as they are. We try to avoid making people who are not on committees feel they do not belong. Their positive presence is seen in other ways. This factor is particularly underlined in funeral liturgies where we give thanks for the accurate specifics of individual witness.

Our pastoral council tries to be a catalyst for the involvement of our voluntary organisations, a promoter of values and a disseminator of our ideas. It strives to be rooted in the ethos and aspirations of each member of the community. We constantly strive to discover our common ideals, our innate culture and the attitudes which determine our daily living. Into each and every aspect we strive to let the light of the gospel shine, particularly in the matter of decision-making. Our gospel vision is rooted in the social fabric and personal freedom and releases the Spirit for development.

Our structure provides for consultation and response, decision and implementation, acceptance with responsibility.

We regard a community as a living organism like a body. Even those aspects which are regarded as closer to the contents of the gut than of the head or heart are part of our agenda. A body cannot exist without a gut that functions!

Our tree of life has a broken branch and it acknowledges some poison in the atmosphere. But it accepts there is more brokenness than poison. Surveys have revealed that four out of five delinquents have difficulties in personal relationships. Much delinquency is a method of achieving legitimate ends by illegitimate means. It is a way of releasing impulses which are otherwise denied. The pastoral council strives to know and hear the voice of God in the signs of the times. Knowing what he wants makes it possible to serve the whole community. His anointing teaches us about everything that is true (1 John 2: 27). Leaders working towards a Christian community of love and sharing often see how they are blessed by God. We evangelise not by numbers, rules or structures, but by love, trusting in him in whom we believe.

The response of people in their houses helps to assess leadership. Is it co-ordination or manipulation? Inviting people to get involved, particularly in one-to-one ministry, has great potential, for example, in caring for single parents, the unemployed, the lonely, the bereaved, the parents of the sick or handicapped. It is full of the most exciting prospects. We know that if anything is developed in a confused way it can have dismal prospects. It cannot be divorced from the people and groups whose individualism has to be respected.

Yet individualism is one of the curses of Irish society. So leadership is needed to draw together diverse ministries. This will not necessarily come about because an action is planned. The best approach will include discussion, reflection and prayer. The Acts of the Apostles is a marvellous source of reflection and inspiration, with regard to our mission as a Church. Yet action is also a great necessity.

The pastoral council is at the heart of our tree. Contact is maintained with all the groups mostly through its main branches. It also conducts inquiries, surveys, and has an ear at our parish assemblies.[5] Action comes through the setting up of new groups for revealed needs: scripture and prayer groups, employment action, education through FÁS for job creation, the housing action group (a Social Employment Scheme), the parents' council and the parish ministry course. There is also liaison with existing groups.

The pastoral council, having a common vision of our Church, helps communicate it in a way that is intelligible to the laity. The members of it help by showing groups and individuals that by their actions they are being Church. It is by availing of the experience of those willing to travel with us on the journey that roles of the laity have begun to emerge. We are on the way to a comprehensive pastoral plan.

Identifying the gifts that God has placed within our community and matching them to the needs that our surveys and visitation have discovered is a primary task of the pastoral council (see Appendix 3). This is not merely a social service. Our experience has been that the needs identified never include anything of a religious or spiritual nature. Social and financial matters dominate the thinking of parishioners about the parish.

Our desire to help every baptised member of the parish to accept that they share in the evangelising mission of the Church meets with apathy or resistance. While the gospel value of building up the community through mutual service evokes a positive response, nourishment for the faith, the rock on which such values stand is often rejected. Yet by availing of their talents, interests and experience in a collaborative way the mission of the baptised has now become part of most parishioners agenda.

IV
AVAILING OF EXPERIENCE

'*You* are afraid to get involved with us. We still don't feel that *we* are the Church. Why are you afraid to let us decide?'

These comments, from some of our more committed laity, are more a comment about Church rules, than about the way we relate as religious, laity and clergy. Lay people keep saying to us priests that we are the ones who are incapable of being involved.

'You are expected to make the decisions finally, from outside or above the lay groups. You won't make them with us or from within. The Church expects the priests or the bishop to make all the real decisions. So how can you risk real involvement?'

Even though that's what lay people say, it's not the whole truth. While the rules of the Church (in Canon Law) give that impression, they are not the only or best way of identifying roles for the laity.

In our visitation of the homes, in meetings of our parish council, in parish assemblies and in surveys of people's priorities in the parish we were 'need-led'. Some surveys dealt with matters like unemployment, social needs, available crafts, skills and services. Other inquiries focused on people's likes and dislikes in the parish.[6] There were surprises. Parishioners were not willing to allow religious or categories of laity, for example, ministers of the eucharist, lead prayer in the home.

Parents' concerns about matters educational was the top priority. As a result we established elected parents' councils in both primary schools.[7] Their primary task, because of anxieties and attitudes revealed, is to keep the elected parents on the board of management in touch with the parents. The parents' response to departmental papers reviewing the curriculums, on discipline and on the government's green paper on education was sought. All the council members received copies of these papers for their reflection. They were asked to respond to other initiatives of the board of management about uniforms, the provision of improved facilities, the desirability of teacher-parent meetings. For the people this was a significant move from consultation to participation.

The parents' council provides parents with information and a home-school link which is based on mutual trust. Councils are not a complaint forum relating to individual children. Such problems are the responsibility of the parents concerned and the child and teacher involved. The parents' council helps to develop and strengthen school-home-parish-community lines of communication, without interfering in the day to day running of the school. The aim is to assist parents in their role as the primary educators of the child.

Many parents regard it as significant that the opinion of the council was sought in drawing up the criteria used by the board for the selection of teachers. Their involvement in the process helped parents to discover that the teacher appointed is not someone who has influence with the priest and that a fair system for getting the best available is scrupulously implemented. It also helped parents to be more appreciative of the calibre and commitment of the teachers appointed and of the caring Christian ethos of the school. The criteria finally formulated by the selection panel looked for a person of integrity who

(i)   respects persons and their dignity and demonstrates a capacity to relate well to colleagues, pupils, authority and parents

(ii)   realises the importance of accountability, co-operation, decisiveness, fairness and justice

(iii)   has a sense of responsibility realised in:

   (a) regular and punctual attendance and fidelity to school regulations

   (b) insistence on the careful observance of rules and the keeping of proper records

   (c) attention to the importance of honest communication at all levels

   (d) awareness of and compliance with the role and function of the board of management

(e) desire for the development, care and safety of each child with adequate supervision at all times

(f) care for the maintenance of school buildings, furniture and equipment, and the proper use of public finance

(iv) has a vision of what could be achieved in the school and how various aspects of school life – curriculum, homework, discipline – might be co-ordinated among the staff and further assisted by dialogue with parents, about matters relating to the education of their children, singly, in groups and with the parents' council

(v) has the essential teaching qualifications and a variety of teaching experience and a willingness to arrange varied extra-curricular events

(vi) Recognises the importance of community in the life of the person and the partnership of Church, parent, and teacher, in the total development of the child

(vii) Has a good moral character and is committed to upholding the religious ethos of our school and community

(viii) Is likely to be acceptable to and be able to work with the present staff

(ix) Will be committed to the good of the school in all its aspects

(x) Is available for interview and accepts these criteria.

In the appointment of a school principal in addition to the above we sought a person with 'an ability to lead, inspire others and delegate'.

The parents council provides a forum for teachers to develop school policy and acquire parental co-operation with regard to school discipline, homework facilities, equipment, workbooks. On one of the councils this has been a great focus for action. In consequence, swimming, educational trips, PE and dancing were added to the curriculum. In addition there is an opportunity for an informed dialogue with regard to 'steamy school gates issues'. Official recognition by the board of management of the council's right to think and act on its own initiative on behalf of the parents who elected them is a great strength. In one of the schools especially parental frustration and sometimes anger have given way to a marvellous partnership.

The parents council are encouraged to advise the pastoral council on initiatives to help the school in its contribution to building a community of living faith.[8] The young grow to appreciate the life and mission of Jesus Christ when they give expression to such faith in their daily lives. When they experience the primacy of love, children recognise the dignity of each person and the humanity and nobility of Christian values. They grow to appreciate the contribution of justice, joy, prayer, peace and the works of the Spirit to the well-being of society.

Our parish pastoral council is especially attentive to the parents council in furthering a collaborative approach to ministry. This 'new form of co-operation between parents and the Christian community, between the various educational groups and the pastors' is a model for helping clergy and religious to decide *with* rather than *for* the laity.

The parish council as an integral part of our collaborative model of Church planned that the parents elected to the board of management be *ex-officio* members of the parents council. This was over-ruled by the patron. Nevertheless, we established a direct link to the board asking the elected parents to liaise between both. This brought the richness of a responsible link to the concerns of parents. Unlike groups established in accordance with the norms of the Code of Canon Law, everyone else has an equal say with the priest on the board.[9] The witness of priests, capable of involvement without expecting 'to make the decisions finally from outside or above the lay group' spoke far more about our new model of being Church to the articulate independent young parents, than a thousand sermons.[10] We all strive to bring that spirit into the groups established according to the hierarchical model of the Code of Canon Law.

Dialogue with the parents deepens our respect for their vocation. Most parents live out their Christian calling much better than they understand. Their personal sacrifices, their faith, their prayer and their willingness to learn for the sake of their children is one of the richest leadership contributions in the Church today.

Such parents are in great need of our support, approval and encouragement. If our homilies or attitudes emphasise the negative, there is merely discouragement. If the future passes by the way of the family there is much goodness upon which to build. Our contact with the needs of people is one of our guiding principles for pastoral action. It is not the only principle. There is more to life than need. Solutions through leadership in accordance with the values of the gospel are the ingredients of our response. We do not tell people what to do from outside their real situation. We share our leadership with the parents. We know their concerns, problems, difficulties and opportunities. Together we look at all of this in the light of the gospel and the hope that it brings.

V
SHARING THE LEADERSHIP

Parents consistently express their bewilderment and sense of aloneness in the face of the brokenness of modern culture. Parents of teenagers have particular difficulties. We addressed some of these in an Easter message of hope in 1992. As usual our approach was ecumenical. The media latched on to a brief reference to *Nighthawks*. Pauline Cronin in the *Sunday World* scoffed at our reference to *Nighthawks* when it finished its 298th show: 'Phew!! the clergy in Castlecomer are really on the ball with their "ecumenical letter to families" giving out about *Nighthawks*.'[11] We saw it as a message of hope. Affirming the special leadership role of parents in society is not guaranteed a good press!

The very help we gave parents became a media ingredient creating the very culture that oppresses them. Our parents reacted positively. They understood our message. They felt that there was appreciation of their best efforts. They began to realise that the unacceptable changes in secular society need not necessarily destroy the future happiness of their children. Our slogan for young and old became, 'There is a better way'. Our message analysed this 'time of great change'. We explained why some of us want even more change. We spoke to those who are upset that 'too much of value is lost by this rush of change'. A majority of people see some change as good and some as bad. We went on to show how we 'see good and bad in our changing Ireland'.

'The most painful change is the real difficulty parents have in communicating their experience and wisdom to the young. Our children are growing up in an Ireland where sadly religion and its inherent wisdom, hope and true joy, is being pushed from the centre of life to the fringes. Too many very necessary truths about a life of happiness now are regarded as old fashioned foolishness by youth idols.

'When violence is glamorised in any way or when self-will becomes an acceptable moral code or sexuality is separated from the person, respect and relationship, where killing is made acceptable by any circumstance, then everyone loses out. There is increasing alarm at the extreme values found in modern rock music culture, where anti-social behaviour such as violence, sex, drugs, alcohol and even satanic worship is glorified. The less obvious forms daily seep into the attitude of children and youth pointing them in the same direction – away from the values of the gospel.

'There is a growing disrespect for many good human values, which are also fundamental Christian ones. Much of the tabloid video culture undermines everything that goes to make a decent person, a faithful Christian and a just and peaceful society. A *Nighthawks* mentality parades much of this modern pagan outlook as progressive and desirable.

'Peer pressure, from a very tender age to be part of this culture has now become a cause of stress for many parents. This pressure plus schools distracted and dominated by the points system and the fear of unemployment, with all its consequent evils, cause many parents to feel helpless and hopeless, isolated and unsupported.

'Millions of pounds are spent on the consequence of family breakdown and the failure of this secular "with-it" culture. As this brokenness increases society faces huge problems providing an ever increasing market for the Tabloid and Video culture. Breaking the cycle of brokenness and addiction against a storm of propaganda becomes a frightening pressure on concerned parents.

'Yet, thank God, we have so many wonderful young people, with a mature and Christian attitude, despite the glorification of the *"Mé Féin"* philosophy. Fortunately, parents too are not alone. Our Christian families are reminded in this Easter season that God is with them. As we meet the risen Jesus anew we see that things were much the same for him. He brought real welcome change and the religious leaders did not like his changes. In rejecting his changes they rejected him. We all know what happened.

'We not only have the company of Jesus but the Church too shares our joys and hopes, griefs and anxieties.[12] We are not isolated and alone. We are a people. We are not an old-fashioned, stuffy backward people, living in the past. We are an Easter people with a message of joy and hope for a broken world. We cannot be silent about this good news.

'The Easter Feast and the community it forms through the life-giving waters of Baptism, provide the answer to all our problems. The deeper our understanding of our own Christian traditions the more meaning is added to life. Religious faith is a strength not a weakness. All who experience being loved themselves know how to love. God is true love. Love like his, and not "lording it over others"[13] is the way to personal freedom and social renewal.

'This God of love gave us a truly great freedom that of making our own decisions and living with the consequences.

Yet he showed us how to rejoice with those who rejoice and to weep with those who weep. He loves and supports us in more ways than we can imagine. All who have a true image of God, parent or priest, young or old, will not be or allow others be anybody's doormat. Who wants to wait at the family table as a slave at a feast for the millionaire or be a "caddy" to every whiff or whim of a self-centred child or parent. No one learns respect or the strength that come from love, by being allowed to use others as a convenience for themselves. This is not the way of justice, truth and love – the foundation of true peace, harmony and constant reconciliation.

'In Church, society and family there is also a welcome change in the way we relate to each other. The absolute power of authority to decide and enforce its will is no longer acceptable. Certain basic rights must now be recognised and respected. Deciding in isolation and issuing orders, merely "drives people to anger and resentment" (be they children, laity, workers, priests, women). Yet giving in or silently standing back to let people do what they like leads to chaos. *There must be leadership.*

'Christian leadership is a very urgent need of modern Ireland. Welcome changes respecting the dignity and freedom of conscience and the integrity of the person, if misused, lead to chaos in society. The child's "I don't want to ..." or a teenager's "I have a right to ...", when they become a stubborn insistence on "getting one's own way" is a subversion of social order, if accepted as normal behaviour. However, dictation, confrontation and condemnation are *not* the way of genuine Christian leadership in family or community.

'Parents have a special leadership role in the family – listening, setting an example, encouraging, supporting, stimulating, challenging, stretching, guiding, depending on the circumstances. In this way, we create an environment in which children learn to become responsible, to develop their fullest potential, change and modify their behaviour, to have a genuine respect. This is also the way they get a true image of the Father, Jesus and the Holy Spirit. As our Churches remind us so often there is only one defence our children have against the bad changes in the modern Ireland – to be steeped in the truths revealed by Jesus.

MEET THE RISEN JESUS:

'When we look at accounts in the scriptures of people recognising the risen Jesus, we often find them in a negative attitude.[14] They were "alarmed", "frightened", "confused", "doubting", "faces downcast", "it was still dark", "weeping", "mourning and in tears", unable to believe unless … Many of our painful confusions if viewed in the light of the Easter story may bring us directly to the risen Jesus. This one action may be the most necessary in the Ireland of today.'

We went on to encourage parents to open *Colliery Christians*, our parish booklet of local happenings. New situations need new remedies. 'New wine needs new wineskins'. But it is important to help our young people to know the difference between wine and wineskin. It is important that we adults put our energy into preserving the one rather than the other.

The death of one of our youth workers soon reinforced all that we had said. Our outreach to the alienated led to a futile search for services.

---

1   Quarterly Bulletin to provide information and documentation from Irish Bishops' Conference, Catholic Press and Information Office.
2   Available from Clogh Parish Council (£2 incl. postage).
3   NCPI opted out of the debate about the appointment of bishops when they 'prudently' substituted silence for response when the right to express their legitimate views was given no respect. (See Chapter 3, Section 4).
4   Cf. O O'Sullivan, 'The Silent Schism', *The Furrow* (Jan 1994) and C Kilcoyne, *The Sunday Press* (9 January 1992).
5   All parishioners are invited to meetings and have an opportunity to speak their minds. The huge attendances limit the effectiveness.
6   See Appendix 3.
7   The association of the Federation of Catholic Primary Schools Parents

Councils, St Patrick's Marino, Griffith Avenue, Dublin 9 was invaluable. They provided wise guidelines and also met parents.

8   Cf. Catholic Primary School Managers Association, *Management Board Members Handbook*, pp 5-13, Veritas (1993).

9   Collins Liturgical Publications, Sydney 1983.

10 See note 3.

11 P. Cronin, 'Telly Views', *Sunday World* (April 1992).

12 *Pastoral Constitution on the Church in the Modern World*.

13 Luke 22: 25; cf. John 13.

14 Luke 24; John 20; Matthew 28.

CHAPTER 6

REACHING OUT TO EVERYONE

I
A SEARCH FOR SERVICE

On 23 August 1992 a young man from our parish died, having been stabbed to death in Kilkenny City. That year our parish had concerned itself about the environment in which our young people were growing up. In addition to the admonitions contained in our Easter message (Chapter 5, Section 5) we had decided to examine it from several points of view.

Alan, the nineteen-year-old who was stabbed, together with his mother and others, had completed a youth leadership training programme during that summer. Alan was the 'hero' figure to the young and we were trying to draw distanced youth back into community and society. His tragic death was mortal in three senses: for Alan, for his parents' family life – he was an only child – and for our community, as he was the keystone of our youth programme.

During the following two weeks we contacted many agencies seeking support in our distress. Many of our young people had become deadly depressed under numerous influences. They indulged in the more unacceptable lyrics of 'Guns and Roses' music. We discovered that there is no psychiatric service for people under eighteen years of age in the entire South Eastern Health Board region. We discovered that there is no service to meet the drugs epidemic. The social worker is sorely stretched interviewing families in crisis. In her forty-hour week she has little opportunity actually to provide a solution for the problem. Apparently we are again dependent on community-based support for caring.

Drugs are as freely available as alcohol at the functions our young people attend. Those over eighteen say that they are too old for some of these functions. Our Easter message attempted to involve the parents in seeking amelioration of the traumatic environment in which our youth are being brought up. Alan's death intensified our experience of helplessness when we discovered the absence of a social policy in relation to youth.

The preoccupation of influential leaders in the Church with practices and values that we claim as essential to our religion are often an obstacle to allowing the innate values of the youth to be acknowledged, appreciated and developed. Their sense of justice, compassion and genuine hunger for equality of dignity are also religious values. Sexual morality based on these values appeals to youth. There is little justification for making the availability of condoms a major moral issue. Adultery or fornication without a condom is hardly more virtuous than adultery using one! This all has relevance to the AIDS and drugs epidemic but is more symptomatic of the human and religious boundaries we have to cross if we are to reach and touch our dying youth.

We read many reports of concerned committees; yet we are convinced that the majority of the state agencies are so far above the surface that they have not begun to scratch it. Those of us in the field need no research or reports to know for example that drugs are available to *all* our children. We know that thirteen- and fourteen-year-olds got them free while at festivals.

The drugs culture thrives in an environment of injustice, weakness, and instability. There is so little at primary school to help the vulnerable. (There is only one remedial teacher in the nineteen schools that link into Castlecomer Community School.) When children are sent to clinics for assessment, the report will be comprehensive. It may speak of dyslexia, impaired hearing (and sight), emotional disturbance (such as that resulting in lack of toilet control, etc.). There is goodwill amongst the teachers to make a positive response to this information but there is nowhere to turn for teaching aids, counselling or space for discussion with parents to respond to the information provided by the assessment. The exercise presumably expensive, has no practical outcome.

The educational structure ought to provide opportunities for linking school, family, and environment in a manner that will be productive for the child's emotional growth, health and happiness. The current government Green Paper is pre-occupied with the person as a unit of economic reproduction. This is to detach work from the person and the person from the complete social context.[1]

In our community we provide leadership training and counselling. We allow our young people to turn an 'adult-only' view of religion and virtue on its head. We have action for employment, a voluntary housing agency for elderly and young marrieds. However, the cultural, economic, and moral climate undermines much of our effort.

We explained how these beliefs became a conviction in a dossier to a minister for community care.[2] We wrote to him because a comprehensive programme integrating the work of five departments is necessary. This already exists for dealing with the drug scene in Dublin. Collaboration with the Churches and voluntary organisations is needed.

We received no response from any national or local state agencies – except from the gardaí who themselves experience similar frustration. When we contacted the National Youth Council[3] and National Youth Federation,[4] they said that lack of funds and inadequate numbers of volunteers deprived them of time and resources to address the social issues. They have now confined themselves to 'Youth Activities'. Nobody seems to care about how many of our young people are dying. At a wedding on the day of Alan's funeral the groom told me that five of his classmates have committed suicide. Six of my nephew's classmates died before his twenty-first birthday. Drug abuse is not merely an inner city problem.

Any kid in this rural parish can obtain drugs. In some instances they get them from those whom the adult community expects to be their protectors. Though they are contributory factors to the accidents and suicides, the young deaths are not the consequence of drugs alone. In our discussions with young people, individually and in groups, we have discovered that many are totally alienated from society.

The idealism of youth dissolves before this cold pragmatism. The social acceptance of milking the system weakens their will to life. Tax evasion/tax avoidance have the same meaning for them. Exploiting the grants system in industry and farming is immoral in the eyes of the young. The search for employment seems futile too. A notional concern for family values has a hollow ring to the young neighbour of the welfare-assisted single parent who in turn is supported by the 'live-in' lover who often is drawing full unemployment benefit while working for an adequate wage totally outside the tax system. Yet these job-seeking unemployed young people cannot get similar subsidised accommodation. Because of their parents tax-ravaged income and because they are still living at home they are rendered ineligible.

They are angry at the bad reputation given to them by the few, whose robbery exploits are well know but not legally provable. Their innate sense of justice, their compassion for the frightened elderly in their homes, their loyalty to and love of family are the constraints which prevent so many of our youth from joining those who always get away with 'everything'.

In these circumstances the God of our Churches has little meaning or relevance. Are they not really hungry to meet the Jesus of the gospel? Why is it that this Jesus with whom youth have no quarrel is concealed and out of reach in the Church as they experience it? The Church too is providing services out of old models in a language the youth do not understand. The vacuum left in society by the collapse of spiritual and moral values can only be filled by their restoration.

For an effective pastoral plan all the social partners including the Churches must make the question of justice a national priority. Arrogantly dismissing the alienated as outcasts who deserve their fate may console the comfortable but will not cure the problem. Our neighbouring island with some 100,000 homeless or runaway children – 30,000 in London alone – remind us that even the welfare state is not the answer. True wisdom comes from the mouths of the Old Testament prophets in their call for justice. Tempered with mercy, justice also is the way of Jesus.

II
A STRUGGLE FOR JUSTICE

One of the difficulties for our Church in promoting social justice as a religious issue is the prejudice of the national context in which it must operate. It is permitted the role of consoler of the wounded and the helper of the homeless. It is seen as a legitimate role of the Church to dispense charity to the poor. However, when it wishes to question and challenge the structures that keep them poor, then its voice is silenced.

In our parish, in co-operation with two neighbouring parishes including the Church of Ireland parish which geographically covers all three, we have begun to take a stand on issues affecting the lives of rural people. They find that life is getting tough – the great frustration is what they call 'the system'. We decided to try to raise the morale of those devastated by a lack of employment prospects.

We identified tourism and ancillary services as a way to create employment. Recognising the necessity of providing accommodation if people are to come and stay in our community, we encouraged private individuals to provide this service.

The people whom I meet who are trying to do something to provide employment are very disillusioned. The Maastricht Millions are regarded as regulation money. Highly paid technocrats make mountains of regulations for which they receive excessive salaries or payments. As a consequence these regulations make the provision of facilities so difficult that the project is no longer viable.

That is the perception of one family who invested a hundred thousand pounds in providing bed and breakfast accommodation. Not one single cent of grant aid was available to them because of 'regulations'. Even to get to know of the regulations demands the hiring of one or other of a team of professionals. They in turn receive excessive fees for their services. My own conscience accuses me of encouraging this good family to trust a system that in one year devoured the hard earned income of their life's work.

The real pain is in the fact that the energy and expense put into coping with the regulations if put into promotion would bring in the tourist. When your life savings are spent on a project the community encourages you to develop and when only two tourists knock at your door in a full year, then rural development loses its gloss.

The Church has an urgent role to play in rural development. What can she do? Why not organise a network of the people for the transformation of the system and culture that oppresses them? From Leo XIII (1891) to John XXIII, Church analysis of the world order was looked at through the eyes of the property owner. Nevertheless, it brought to the forefront of social policy the concept of a 'living wage' and an awareness that human beings are more important than structures. Our 1937 constitution framed on the principle that the state should not do what a lesser body can do is now devoid of that social and moral force. Meanwhile from Pope John XXIII onwards, and particularly through the influence of Pope Paul VI the Church was realising that systems favour one group above another. Church policy began to urge political activity in the care of the disadvantaged. The most profound change brought by Paul VI was the way to progress. 'Social teaching' was to be replaced by reflection and action on people's real life situation.

Our parish council strives to give a vision of the essential elements in being truly human in the modern context. We first get people to look at life as it is lived. Having seen the awesome extent of pain present in poverty, unemployment, homelessness, emigration we start asking questions. Why are rural areas neglected by the economic-political structures? Why are the professionals paid ten times the income of the ordinary person in the countryside to tell him to take all the risks in creating employment?

We sent the following letter to all the national newspapers in September 1991. Not one of them published it. We issued a sort of Trotskyite challenge to institutional tyranny as follows:

'Our national rhetoric speaks of equality of dignity, human rights, shared responsibility, and freedom with moral accountability . We Irish claim a style of leadership that is consultative, collegial and responsive to a moral democratic philosophy of life. We claim two-way communication as integral to our culture, rules, roles, beliefs, values, norms and structures. All our power structures presuppose a mutual accountability.

'The reality is in stark contrast to the rhetoric, in almost every facet of Irish society. We Irish tolerate a controlling, enforcing, authoritarian, legalistic leadership style. Communication channels transmit unilateral decisions downwards only. Accountability patterns merely go upwards to the boss. All our top people are remarkably free of accountability. We give priority of protection even in law and legal precedents to the institution and its boss.

'Subservience to institutional injustice thrives in Ireland. "Loyalty" is more valued than moral accountability. Fear and insecurity are sufficient to permit 'the boss' to do it his way. Total alienation seems the inevitable consequence. There is very little concrete action to resolve this conflict between the reality and our rhetoric. This is true everywhere, from lay involvement in Church, through politics to the allotment of admission tickets in sports organisations.

'We the people, are accomplices if we opt out, when

structures permit involvement and a share in decision making. We are very subservient shareholders, club members, delegates to organisations, party branch members, priest and lay members of Church groups, etc.

'Our Parish Pastoral Council identified a huge variety of injustices which apparently enjoy the privilege and protection of the law. We, the members, are hoping that out of the current crisis, institutional changes capable of turning the rhetoric into reality might emerge. We ourselves have been victims of institutional violence.[5]

'We need to insist that the norms, roles and culture barriers be smashed particularly by those who have the resources, and the authority to effect change. Leadership must replace reaction. The law makers must provide institutions of justice. Enquiries and Ritual Resignations are a mere beginning,' we concluded.

Pelvic politics have replaced the hunger for justice, freedom and the patriotic endeavour on which our political parties were founded. They no longer analyse and respond to the strengths and weaknesses in our society. The demise of active party branches through which political leaders might listen to the grassroots together with their imprisonment in the mentality mentioned in paragraph two of the letter above leaves a huge vacuum which could well be filled by anarchy/revolution or creative leadership.

The Church is still one of the strongest forces for the transformation of rural Ireland. It not only provides a comprehensive process but can help the elimination of unilateral decisions. It can campaign to make the top people subject to accountability. If a bench of bishops goes to Brussels as a contribution to two-way communication we are encouraged. They can be part of the voice from the bottom. They, like community radio and local newspapers, can reflect the reality. Their contact with a variety of social action groups and development organisations by means of parish councils creates an awareness of the questions involved. From this practical social analysis, real solutions might begin to emerge.

Politicians too must pay more attention to those in touch with the reality than to media commentators.[6] They will begin to realise that the real social agenda for the ordinary person concerns questions of survival, justice and dignity.[7] The 'works of mercy' and social welfare solutions while a necessity at the level of human need, are the answers from an age of paternalism, when the dignity of the person especially of the poor was not a social priority. Community development and rural renewal, require that a little of the Maastricht millions by-pass the overpaid technocrat and his bureaucratic disciples. Only then can a 'bottom-up' policy be a reality rather than rhetoric.

As an instrument for action we set up the Colliery Christians Voluntary Housing Association, the North East Kilkenny Development Association and its local sub-group the Colliery Development and Heritage Committee. *The Colliery Christians Magazine* was a voice for the emigrant and the unemployed. We urged the County Development Team, the Rural Tourism Development Committee to help change the system. Up to five or six years ago county councils were supportive agencies for the average person. Now initiatives coming from Brussels via Dublin have brought the 'top-down' hide-bound by rules and regulations mentality almost to the bottom. With all this oppressive weight on top of us at the bottom, the highly paid technocrats are now telling us that the solution is a 'bottom-up' approach.

However, this approach is doomed to failure if implemented with a boss mentality. To subject the proposals from the bottom to the regulations from the top is merely to complete the total crushing of the local initiatives.

Ultimately, a proper understanding of the gospel will be needed if everyone is to be freed from the apathy into which the system has crushed them. It could also profitably stir the anger of the victims and channel it into positive action.

The new collaborative way of being Church is a potential social revolution, a powerful social force for the defence of human dignity and for freedom from rejection and alienation. The inter-Church collaboration in our parish is such a force for co-ordination and motivation that a new style of leadership has emerged. A consultative, collegial, responsive leadership root-ed in a moral and democratic philosophy of life is beginning the revolution. The fight is on for equality of dignity and opportunity. The days of subservience are ending. A new justice and peace group (again interdenominational) will provide the analysis and leadership. The Church in Ireland, twenty years after the radical changes brought by Paul VI, is now becoming part of the revolution. This Church in rural Ireland is its hope for the future as well as being a more accurate reflector of the values of the gospel of Jesus Christ.

III
RENEWING OUR BROKENNESS

The social implications of the welcome emancipation of women, may be volcanic. Jack Dominian in the Christmas 1992 edition of the *Tablet* gave some social and psychological reasons for a mammoth increase in the breakdown of marriage. This marriage expert with vast counselling experience draws our attention to the quest in western society for emotional and sexual fulfilment. In the west there is a craving for equality of loving, emotional availability and the need for affirmation. How do we provide for this?

The Child Care Act was implemented only as a result of public pressure after highly emotional events.[8] British and US studies show the social and emotional disturbance of children from broken homes. 'Even more serious, the future marriages of those who come from broken homes have a much higher incidence of marital breakdown. Adolescent girls from broken homes are more promiscuous and are more likely to become pregnant after extra marital relationships with high rates of abortion.' For adults too there is evidence of post-break-up depression, shock, distress, alcoholism and even suicide according to Dr Dominian in the article cited above.

The social havoc of marital breakdown is already beginning to affect us. It will multiply, adding significantly to the workload of the caring Christian community. The state will not help. There is absolutely no action whatever as a result of the recent social legislation. Local communities will have to pick up the pieces. The importance of knowledge of personal relationships as offered by the Clare and Limerick youth services should be an essential element to all education.[9] Lifeskills can only be learned and evaluated, not taught.

Is there as much understanding of the agony as of the ecstasy of love? The potential for joy in true love is our gift for the world. The tabloids' superficiality is destructive of the essential aspects of our journeys from isolation, loneliness, and alienation. The chemical attraction between a pair who are each others 'need-meeters', is not true love – even if accompanied by a super sexual expression of physical and emotional availability!

To be fully awake, fully alive and truly living is more than a thing of the emotions. How to savour the real, touch the vulnerability and fragility of the heart, the sensitivity of the spirit, of every person is a human and spiritual journey. Real love takes us beyond the fantasies to a real person with prejudices, desires, compulsions, addictions, negativities as well as 'divine' qualities. Real love brings delight and dread.

The best Christian gift towards creating a new Ireland is a love in touch with the interior that is more decision than emotion. This contribution of a Christian marriage cannot be imposed. Now that the state has established its independence of the Church and vice versa it might start co-operating as partners in the service of love and peace An extract from our letter to all the national Papers (again not published) after Mother Teresa's visit is still valid. Having praised the Lord Mayor's speech we went on to explain why we see the polarisation between bishops and politicians as corrosive of the moral fibre of society and detrimental to the maturity and life of our youth.[10]

'The disintegration of the moral fibre of our society is a serious and frightening prospect as present trends indicate. Church/State separation is a sensible expression of pluralism and cultural diversity. Church/State conflict is eroding the bonding elements in the truly human values which in Catholic terms we express as the gifts and fruits of the 'spirit'.

'On human dignity, on real love and its significance in human affairs, on justice at home and abroad, rural development, urban renewal, work as the key to fulfilment, on emigration and homelessness, the hierarchy seem closer to the people. In areas of personal freedom, the implications of pluralism on the individual traumas (too much publicised?), the politicians have the edge in closeness to people.

'A public perception that politicians, for example, regard promiscuity as a modern (progressive) and acceptable lifestyle undermines qualitative relationships. This has fearful consequences for the fabric of society. A perception by youth that the bishops see it as less sinful to transmit Aids while fornicating, than to use a condom, distorts the beauty and truth of the core of the Catholic social and moral vision of human dignity.

'Our vision of life and the ingredients for social cohesion and human happiness have diminished rapidly during the fifteen year liberal-conservative collision. With many human and social dilemmas still to be resolved a new approach by Church and State leaders is a necessity. A shared vision is essential for human dignity, freedom, justice and responsibility in personal and human development. This is possible if we utilise the insights of those whose caring is practical rather than ideological.

'As a Church we ought to return again to that true spirit of Vatican II. As a society can we develop the momentum of the process started by the honouring of Mother Teresa and the accompanying tributes to the contribution of religious to our society's well being? It has shown the national politicians that it is worth the risk to hear the perspective of a real carer.[11] Campaigns "driven" by hidden negatives like anger, envy or revenge possess the wrong spirit.

'The return of this prophetic little Nun to the place where she "first learned to love Jesus" – the novitiate of the Loreto Sisters at Rathfarnham, may yet have richer consequences for Ireland than a papal visit.[12] But only if all of us together are willing to tease out its significance and have access to a responsible means of publicly sharing our perspectives.'

Our request for a debate on the significance of the visit was denied a public airing. The dogmatism of ideology – be it liberalism, capitalism, feminism, marxism, fundamentalism – never identifies with the aspirations and anguish of ordinary people. It is only people – neighbour to neighbour – who are ultimately able to love and respect as equals those from whom they differ in colour, class and creed. If this love is to come from an interior life and flow from what is best in the human spirit, spiritual direction is needed. New models of ministry and appropriate training for those opting for the new ministries is an urgent necessity. Otherwise we remain prisoners of dogmatism. 'New Age' is a growth industry revealing a spiritual hunger worldwide. Spiritual direction; Taize events; meditation both from east and west and their fusion; the development of the relationship with God for those reaching the fifth and sixth stages of the spiritual journey all reveal a need in Ireland for a spirituality centre. So many broken lives are really in need of a redeeming force. Christianity provides the intimate confidential sharing which heals.

The word *communio* is used to describe the deepest relationships of which we are capable as humans. *Communio* is a central structural concept in ecclesiology for Anglicans and the Orthodox Churches too. The concept is crucial to Church unity talks – the *communio* of man with God as the foundation for the fellowship of mankind with one another in Christ. It provides the bonding within the diversity of local Churches. The spirit of our times too is developing the authoritativeness of the *communio fidelium*. This gives new emphasis to the *sensus fidei* or *sensus fidelium* where all the members share responsibility in and for the Church.

In training the faithful to use their diversity of gifts to serve a rapidly fragmenting society we need radical new ways of preparing for ministries. Unity and diversity in the Church are equally fundamental. The *sensus fidelium* no longer accepts the centralised authoritarian style discipline of the Vatican curia. Even the bishops are starting to admit that it is not the most faithful presentation of the communio-ecclesiology of Vatican II.

The Christian family is emerging as a more exact model of Church and where true *communio* is more authoritatively presented. The community style Church now emerging needs the collaborative experience of the open marriage. The domestic Church may be taking over from the clericalist one as the channel for transmitting God's 'first gift to those who believe' (Eucharistic Prayer 4). The shortage of vocations to the priesthood may be the work of the Holy Spirit. The spirit of love may want to encourage us to train and involve the lay faithful for the work of spiritual direction and faith development.

IV
THROUGH THE CHRISTIAN FAMILY

The Spirit comes to help us in our weakness (Rom. 8: 22). Releasing the Spirit's power in the hearts and lives of the people of God animates renewal in a manner that cannot be accomplished by a preoccupation with its institutional and orthodox dimensions. Our recent seminar on the Spirit renewed faith and joy in a significant way. However, despite all our efforts we are still only scratching the surface. How do we get all parishioners dare their 'yes' and experience a meaning and respect their 'yes' so that all things acquire meaning to paraphrase Dag Hammerskjold.

The Christian family is basically a witnessing community, built on faith, calling the world to the noblest value of true love imaginable. This is a challenge to our baptismal practice. Can we baptise without the Christian community and before the faith of the family is renewed? Is it fair to ask people to promise to raise their child in the faith if they are left with very deficient images of Church, life, sacraments, Jesus and God? Baptism gives people a right to the other sacraments; yet we lay down laws about participation in the others, for example, the eucharist, priesthood and inter-Church marriage. Is not baptism without faith the real scandal?

The baptised are the gifted people of God. If we do not change our practice at the crucial point of entry, people will never stop to discover and commit themselves to the whole new conciliar meaning of Church. Baptism in each parish once per year and in its proper paschal context would awaken the whole community. A rite of welcome for the child, a renewal programme for parents and preparation of the welcoming Easter community would be helpful in redirecting our minds. Movement from a maintenance to a mission model of Church would help the parish discover its responsibility for the faith and mission of those accepted for baptism.

Renewal of confession is also an urgent need if the family is to have the help of the sacrament of reconciliation in renewing its brokenness. This is an area filled with old images, attitudes and practices. In my seminary days the offence, judgement and reparation procedure had more in common with civil judicial conduct than with Christ's treatment of Zacheus (Luke 19: 1-10). At that same time reports from Vatican II were exciting us about freedom of conscience, personal responsibility and social obligation all receiving their ethos from the gospels. The way of Jesus, more curative than corrective, was to draw us to see that sinful choices are hidden deep in our physical, psychological, mental and spiritual being. A mere ritual of confessing and absolution is an inadequate expression of reconciliation as witnessed by the life and death of Jesus and 'the ministry of the Church.'[13]

Renewal for the person as well as *aggiornamento* for the Church calls for a profound adjustment to our mental outlook. Who guides our steps in a way that is compatible with the human experience and the gospel stories?

For a time the thinking of Vatican II on reconciliation was a priority. The priest was encouraged to be a soul-friend aware of his own frailties. This was to lead him to act for Christ, as a brother mediating compassion, understanding companionship and helping to create a climate conductive to the nobler values. God's unconditional love of the sinner gained in prominence. The pilgrim journey was more important than the isolated acts. The life of the sinner was being brought to the God of mercy. The confessional room signalled a more personal approach.

Within a few years most had returned to a tempered version of the old practice. Many people stayed away. At a retreat, Peace in Christ, in Kilkenny, a layman Jean Vanier connected with, touched and accepted my vulnerability and brought the pain of my failure to the God of mercy. His God knew I could not change myself. How was I to grow into Christ? Could I trust his God to take me beyond my compulsions, anxieties, weakness, projection and all the other ways we protect ourselves from knowing the whole truth of our sinfulness? I was freed to see too how our reactive, unaware, responses affect others in calling forth their sin. The person rising above darkness is freed both to accept and give God's love. Then the good in others is brought into prominence. The spirit of love in family life is much more than the union of the flesh. The bonding of a will, mind and heart is only possible with a love that images God.

All three rites of penance need to be used with a conciliar spirit if the sacrament is to be a process of reconciliation and an instrument of renewal for family and Church.[14] Using the third rite as a mere ritual will reinforce the sin/absolution mentality of pre-Vatican II days. In the journey of on-going conversion we still need to tell our story. Modern secular practice indicates the need to name our sin and see its consequence. With someone to listen, discern and respond we find a solution and healing. But people need to experience mercy and understanding in order to be able to tell their story.

Some of the baptised are blessed with great gifts of listening and helping people past their self-justification, projections and defence mechanisms. Should their gifts not be identified, released and utilised for this ministry? The unity could be provided by the priest in a celebration of reconciliation and absolution. The sacraments should at least make allowance for the human process, allowing the sinner to discover mercy first. The experience of Christian couples and how they are most effectively reconciled should have a more significant influence on pastoral practice.

The question then arising is: where does the spirit work, in Vatican officials or in local Christian communities? If the goal of collaboration is to discover ways to identify, release, utilise and unify the gifts of all baptised Christians can it really be done from a distance? The current retreat from the implications of collegiality and the intensive reinforcement of centralism may frustrate the best effort of the Spirit-filled local faith community. Spirituality centres may also be the best institutions for identifying, releasing and unifying the gifts of the baptised. Collaboration itself may be the very action of the Spirit unifying diversity in one communion of love.

Our self awareness and human development programmes such as the Enneagram are all part of the journey to the relevance that is necessary for a good penitential liturgy. If we truly reverence all people and all things we won't use them for our own needs. Sin twists for its own end. Love reverences all. Beyond the ritual is the relationship. It must be authentic. For that we need to know ourselves and God.

We all need guidance if our human journey is to have that acceptable balance between noise and quiet, wildness and discipline, feast and fast, personal freedom and community responsibility. Some are not suitable for certain tasks. Yet each of us are gifted as singular human beings. We need to be committed to the process of acquiring the necessary skills and the spirituality that will nurture and maintain the core spirit of collaboration. This is true of social, family and liturgical activity.

Meanwhile much of what we do is far from perfect. Some having adjusted to living life addictively are still lifeless on the fringes. They are victims of what our tree (see p. 43) calls poison. But it is only as we become fully alive ourselves will we call them back to life. Immersed in the superficialities of tabloid journalism their understanding is neutralised by over-indulgence in emotionalism.

When we bring people to see and touch the resurrected Christ, life's dilemmas start to fade and dissolve. Some find the love of Christ for others difficult to accept. We must discover from within, through love, that no matter how obnoxious some might seem to us God loves them. Then we are entering more deeply into the meaning of Church. We are also seeing the person as an emotional body and someone with a heart to know and the will to do.

V

SHARING THE FULLNESS OF LOVE

The open Christian family is the richest model of Church at the level of parish. It radiates love and reconciles the alienated. A parish has no strict rules or tight structure. It is a place where law can more easily follow life. It is easier to have fundamental principles enabling the whole people of God to be Church. It is a place where no one has the power to make life conform to law.

Is it not *the* place, therefore, to build a community that is really empowered by love? Like adults in their own home, parishioners come and go in freedom. The love to be found there is basically unconditional. It is a suitable model for the more mature stages of religious growth. In an increasingly secular culture with its corresponding hunger for meaning, we can make allowance for all the diversity of which humans are capable.

In our new age of freedom, we still strive to provide a light in darkness, hope in pain and joy in the gift of life. With real love as the core, a Christian community draws people towards freely chosen commitment. Fidelity in essentials, in the oneness and security of having Christ as head, purifies love.

Family life and married love have to be the most effective channels through which God communicates himself in love today. It is there that all the love of which we have spoken is to be found in its human and spiritual excellence. Narrow, closed, possessive/obsessive rulebound families do not show the love of God as revealed in Jesus.

Traditional emphasis on the procreative nature of marriage tends to move its sacramental focus away from the relational nature of the Blessed Trinity. Our homilies stress that special quality which a Christian love brings to human life. People need help to feel that marriage is the sign of the relationship between God and his people and between Christ and the Church. Celibate love should also reflect this quality of commitment if it is not to deteriorate into detachment.[15]

A genuine response involves a deepening commitment – not detachment. Love is not just pre-creative. It is creative. It promotes growth, strength and wholeness. This centring in love becomes centring in him who is love. The heart and soul of the family is its real witness to the nature of God. Such love will open to the Spirit cells for the future and be rooted in the customs and traditions of history. In this context the authoritative voice of conscience must be primarily in the family. The plans of a family should be made by its members alone as in the Anglican and Orthodox Church. The fruits of the Spirit and his gifts will flow in abundance.

Making burdens too heavy to carry is not recommended by Christ to people in authority (cf. Matt. 23). If life's journey is too steep or painful we become increasingly aware of ourselves. We need breaks to cease being centred on self. Then we can take in and be open to the surrounding beauty. There is more to life than duty.

This is how I see the priest in the local community. With the help of enough cells of love, he will be listening, learning, sharing, hearing the story. He will be inviting rather than converting or subverting, be committed rather than detached. He will rejoice in the pluralism and diversity. He will look beyond jealousy or bitterness or condemnation. He helps resist the pressure that may seek conformity. He helps each to be fully free. Is not this a fatherly role?

The father of community needs daily time to leave the community activity for the silence of the presence. Parents quietly nourished by spousal love expend it on their children. The spiritual father has a similar call – to the lord, as John Paul II reminded us on his visit to Ireland. We return to enjoy a fully human loving relationship with friends who affirm, empower and collaborate in utilising diverse gifts in the cells of love. They too will need continuing training and development to keep drawing forth the love within and utilising it to serve those most in need. A skilful, committed Christ-centred leadership team will provide the necessary inspiration for knowing the truth, affirming faith and discerning God's call to action.

I know that the heart of my Christianity has to be a personal, rather than dutiful, love of Jesus and his brothers and sisters. Yet that calls me to a kind of contemplative prayer. Is this beyond an ordinary mortal? How can I be so attentive and respond to the lord's love that I know my work is his? In *Lumen Gentium* the responsibilities of lay Christians, clergy and bishops are presented within the context of the mission of the Church. The bishops' priestly role put the emphasis on authority as service rather than domination. Those who have authority in the Church are to sanctify, teach and govern a people to whom God communicates himself in love. But all are given the task of fellowship, ministry and witness. Ecumenical friends claim that the discussions at the Third General Assembly of the World Council of Churches at New Delhi (1961) centred on these three biblical terms.

How does the servant of a people to whom God communicates himself in love, authoritatively connect the cry of humanity with the love pouring out of the heart of Jesus? Do we who disturb the universe by our egotism not bring this to Jesus at the start of mass? Do we start annihilating the ego by attuning our minds to the mind of Christ in the readings? We offer ourselves for enlightenment. Scripture group membership helps a few to break away from the mind of the crowd. So too do parents sharing the prayer and scripture in the child's religion book. However, for most people this part of the mass goes over their head. There is much work to be done in explaining, interpreting, hearing the scripture. Our Seminar in the Spirit set many in the right direction. The work of sanctifying, teaching and governing are parts of a cyclic whole. This work is best accomplished in the divine presence. Our tradition demands a special place for this most sacred meeting – God's house.

My cousin was an altar boy in Grogan near Rathdowney, County Laois. He took us inside the altar rails. I went into shock for a couple of days. I was taught well. It was a terrifying thing to enter the sanctuary of God. It was a sin to speak in Church. Reverence in God's house made it a sacred space for God alone. Throughout the Bible we see the necessity of the sacred place where God meets his own – the desert, 'a quiet place all by Himself', the mountain, the wilderness, the temple and synagogue. The Church has always seen these biblical experiences as a mirror of our interior journey. In all these places when trials or bewilderment abounded, God abounded even more.

Some say our liturgies are drama, even entertainment; or they pander to the self-centredness of people. We hope that they are a meeting-point between us in our trials or bewilderments and God who is always near. We know that God is the focus of good liturgy. Our liturgies strive to direct ourselves and others into the deepest presence of God.

Faith carries many on to the sacred meeting through consecration and communion. Those who can grasp that holy communion is the most intimate union we can have with God on this earth are transformed into Christ and are one with God. Simultaneously united with all God's people we are the *pobal Dé* – his Body. We have also touched a unity that is promised and found in love. This is the ultimate orthodoxy. It is here we know that, 'The Church is home and family for she opens wide her doors and welcomes all who are alone or abandoned; in them she sees the specially beloved children of God whatever their age, aspirations, difficulties or hopes.'[16]

In a family setting we live out 'that self-giving love which is capable of accepting those who are different, making their needs and demands its own and allowing them to share in its own benefits. The domestic virtues, based upon a profound respect for human life and dignity and practised in under- standing patience, mutual encouragement and forgiveness, enable the community of the family to live out the first and fundamental experience of peace, joy and love.'[17] 'If love is not revealed to him, if he does not experience it and make it his own, a love that is an intense and enduring moral force which seeks the good of others, even at the cost of self-sacrifice then life is senseless.'[18] 'The human being remains a being that is incomprehensible to himself outside the context of affectionate relationships and of fruitful mutual solidarity.'[19]

Our vision and mission is a pastoral plan based on the family as the primary agent of renewal. Our context is the unique communion of persons united in love, rooted in him 'from whom every family in heaven and earth is named' forming a holy communion through our eucharistic celebration of redemption. We see love as the most authentic mirror of the Holy One who made us in his image and redeems our love of its self-centredness (Eph. 3: 15). Our belief in God is the unique context for our solidarity and belonging. Through him, with him and in him, we are his unique communion of service journeying in hope of love and glory and life eternal.

---

1   This inspired debate throughout the country about the content and control of education. There was much concern about the apparent over-emphasis on education's part in economic development.

2   Chris Flood, a junior minister for health in the Fianna Fáil/Progressive Democrat government (1991–2). He was chairman of a special drugs crisis committee.

3   The co-ordinating council for all bodies dealing with youth

4   An interdenominational co-ordinating body of regional services to young people.

5   A conman fraudulently obtained the signature of the parish priest. He borrowed £4000 from a leasing company and disappeared. The company insisted that the parish was not only liable for the £4000 but also obliged to pay the interest accruing over the three-year period of the lease.

6   When we sent a file on the confidence trick played on us (with special emphasis on the reaction of the company in insisting on our paying for their mistake) we got no reply!

7   Cf. Irish Episcopal Conference, *Work is the Key*, Veritas (1992)

8   Introduced in 1993 to implement Task Force on Child Care recommendations and as a follow-up to the McGuinness Commission on the Kilkenny incest case (See Appendix 4).

9   Limerick Youth Services, Glenworth Street, Limerick.

10 Gay Mitchell at the conferring of the freedom of the city of Dublin on Mother Teresa of Calcutta in June 1993.

11 There was much comment in Ireland that Mother Teresa was not invited to address parliament lest she should oppose the 'liberal agenda' of the government.

12 Mother Teresa's words to Sr Mary O'Kane, the Loreto provincial.

13 From the prayer of absolution.

14 Cf. *Introduction to the Rite of Penance*, Irish Episcopal Conference and Sacred Congregation for the Sacraments and Divine Worship (1976)

15 See 'Priestly Development in a Changing World', Papers of the 1990 AGM of NCPI, Dominican Publications.

16 Message of John Paul II on Day of World Peace (1 January 1994).

17 *Ibid*.

18 John Paul II, *Redemptor Hominis*.

19 See note 16.

CHAPTER 7

THE PARISH PRIEST

I
BEING HUMAN TO BE PASTORAL

The culture of 'control' in Irish society is collapsing. In many of our major institutions and in the Church people are no longer accepting dictation from above or live their lives according to others' expectations. The accompanying loss of authority is forcing many leaders within these institutions to use their power to regain control. The more they exercise this power the greater the loss of authority. The battle and tensions flowing from this makes our work as priests all the more difficult. Providing guidance and wisdom for people who are dis-illusioned, confused and lost is an enormous challenge. Traditionalists and cynics may feel that our approach is the cause of the confusion and alienation. However, forcing people to conform to the traditional values expected by many in society, undermines the possibility of reaching those who no longer accept a control model for living.

Yet much of the culture as reflected in the media is alien to what is good for human development. I refer in particular to our current culture of drink, drugs, crime and faith in the occult. In the area of faith, the old wineskins and the old wine too are regarded by many as totally discardable. As Christians we are striving to find new wineskins for the new wine of a renewed gospel way of living.

Law and order has collapsed at a time when there is an ever increasing demand for the strengthening of laws, greater consistency in their application and more severe penalties for their violation. But the real problem is an interior rejection of law and order. Nobody wants to be told by others how they are to live their life. 'What right have they to ...?' is a regular question whether about laws on marriage or the priest giving sermons. At the same time, we are making mountains of regulations about many other matters; about seat-belts, no smoking zones, the naming of housing estates, planning permissions, rules for receiving grant aid and so on. If we could understand why a person would happily accept a regulation about wearing a seat-belt while resenting regulations about abortion, we would be touching the core of the dilemma facing those who preach good news today.

Part of the rejection of the culture of control is to reject the old style of confessions and preaching though perhaps we do an injustice to the *Sensus Fidelium* to assume that people are rejecting the sacrament of penance or the place of a homily in our faith development.

The hungers in the human heart are unchanging. The values in the gospel are still a new wine that sparkle with attractiveness for the people we meet in our daily work. Yet a service focused exclusively on programmes, on a preoccupation with administration, and accountability according to the standards of a controlling society is rejected.

Both Church and state fear engaging with the new culture. They are tempted to work only with those willing to conform. Yet the real challenge is in establishing meaningful contact with all who have been made inaccessible by this new culture. Our temptation is to deal with that which is safe rather than visionary

One of the great excitements of being a priest in the 1960s in Ireland was the fact that prophets were given an honoured place within the institutions of Church. It is unfortunate that appointments of bishops are now being made by the Curia in a control rather than servant model.

In our rapidly changing Irish society, the loss of confidence in the leaders of our communities is one of the gravest problems facing us today. Without a dynamic and accepted style of leadership, it is nigh impossible to create dialogue and participation. The work of promoting the dignity of people and trying to instil human values into today's culture was never more necessary.

The time has come to focus upon the dignity of the person as the core of our moral concern, both in our Christian and civil life. This demands a renewed commitment to truth, justice and integrity. It means the pain of facing up to a policy of putting truth before loyalty, honesty before appearances, courage before convenience, people before power, affirmation before condemnation, innovation before caution.

We priests need to be open to the new call for freedom of responsibility, to the harnessing of the idealism which is a natural ingredient of youthfulness and to youth's critique of our hypocrisy. We need to give an honoured place again to the prophet and the visionary. We ought to be prepared to change the laws of Church and state, where they diminish the growth and dignity of the human person. We must be honest enough to accept that such laws do in fact exist, particularly in the use of power as a means of control.

Priests are among the true carers in Irish society. Its well-being depends upon them. It is they who teach people how to cope. If their work was successful crime, drug abuse and dabbling in the occult would diminish. Priests hunger for the courage and the resources, human and financial, to make contact with people in the social context of their misguided lives. They search for people of skill and commitment to reach out to our young people, to redirect them towards true happiness and fulfilment. This work demands lay involvement but the lay culture today will refuse to accept the control style of leadership.

In a time of scarce resources, we need to be inventive and inspiring, radical and daring in our plans and attitudes. Why not for example as a signal of a whole new attitude, invite all the prisoners in our jails to sign a declaration that they are willing to change their ways and release them from prison? The resources spared could then be directed to the people committed to help find them a niche and a dignity within society. Prison is much more costly. A further incentive could be an acceptance in their declaration that if they fail to honour that commitment they would have to fully serve out the sentence.

All of this presupposes an ability in the priest to have loving relationships and a capacity for intimacy. The 1990 Annual General Meeting of the National Conference of Priests of Ireland looked at this issue in the context of Priestly Development in a Changing World.[1] The main speaker was international consultant psychiatrist, Jack Dominion. He set the tone of the conference by stating that at the centre of the Christian life lay a unique quality by which all else was to be judged; that was our ability to be loving persons. The conference tried to tease out how celibate priests could have loving relationships, 'the most esteemed characteristics of the human level' and what he called 'the most validating elements of the Christian faith' as taught by scripture.

Fr Brendan Hoban said that seminary formation had provided him with various mechanisms for celibacy – some comical and some absurd – but it didn't envisage loving relationships with other human beings as an important part of his celibacy. 'I and those who shared my training programme are programmed to distrust the heart,' he said. Fr Pat Collins who gives courses in human development, stressing the need for intimacy, said that men in general have difficulty with intimacy. He quoted current research that eighty-seven out of a hundred men in the US never experienced intimacy and he felt things in Ireland were probably the same. Research showed that women had more friendships than men and that there was a marked difference in the content and quality of their relationship. For example, three out of four single women had no problem in identifying a best friend and almost always that person was a woman. He went on to say that if priests were to have the kind of intimacy, which was an honest disclosure of feelings and experiences, they need intimacy with women, who are the experts.

The whole purpose of being intimate was that it put us in touch with our inner lives and hidden selves. It was feelings which told us what we really perceived, thought and valued. He felt that the change from being a role-playing person to a person who 'placed love at the centre of his reality' was crucial for the Church.

The centre of gravity in Catholicism today is shifting from the experience of religious authority to the authority of religious experience. In other words the boss no longer had the influence he had. Only loving persons could help people to interpret a genuine religious experience.

Bishop Laurence Forristal of Ossory who represented the Irish hierarchy at the conference, complimented the priests on the sensitivity and graciousness with which they had dealt with an important and sensitive subject. He would be making a report to his fellow bishops in Maynooth. He would encourage them to consult with delegates who had attended the conference in order to devise ways of bringing the message to all priests. Conference president, Fr Harry Bohan said the model of Church which operated before the Vatican Council would not be appropriate to the 1990s and the twenty-first century. The council had provided the outline of a renewed Church and they would soon have to take deliberations and decisions on board. He appealed to priests and laity to confront the pain of change, to tackle the future rather than be tackled by it. He saw the strength of the future priest as relying on his humanity rather than in presiding.

Our vocation was never described as a call to become men of love. Somehow, we learned that message in our families only. Within a year of ordination I was refused permission to attend my uncle's funeral. This symbolised for me how Church discipline so often interrupts the good because those who made the rules were operating entirely cerebrally. The heart was suspect. If women had a share in devising programmes to create men of love the contribution of family would be seen as an integral part and not an enemy of the process. Is it not impossible to be pastoral with a heart-to-heart concern for others, if love does not flow from our innermost intersection where the enriching intimacies of life meet? We cannot be pastoral if we are not first persons. The authoritativeness of the family is the most appropriate context for pastoral planning. We learn to be Church rather than be in Church by being family – persons interconnected by love. Intimacy rather than control is the way to that sacred interconnectedness.

II
THE PROPHETS OF LOVE

What is it about Mother Teresa of Calcutta that brings out the best in people? She takes us to the very centre of the Christian life. She unfolds the unique quality by which all else is to be judged. What is more esteemed than true love at the human level and at the spiritual level?

A true lover sees beauty and joy everywhere. The true lover is never bored but rejoices in the flower and in life. The true lover has no desire to possess, to dominate, to rape; is not broken and dark but lovable. Without access to the lover in each of us we are cold, not seeing the beauty in the individuality of all things. Real love transforms the unlovable. It opens all to love. Ritual ceremony, law, the orthodox, the moral, and lecturing leave us cold. The one with the contemplative insight, who has discovered love, will never become addicted to the chief substitutes for love; lust, being busy, gathering possess-ions ('my' car, 'my' house) the pseudo joy that the commercials offer us.

God himself has placed in each of us a hunger for love – for the infinite love that he himself is. We miss that target so often because in our struggle to make sense of life we opt for the false joy. We are like dry soil, parched for the rain. We long to be soaked with the word that gives life. We need to receive the word in a manner that is easily understandable to our contemporary mind. We need to move from self-delusion to a genuine experience of religion.

I once shared a house with a simple, humble and contemplative priest. He was a lover in the gospel sense. The comment made about him: 'that his God was God', opened my mind to the core of the prophetic message. Here was a man who was seen to speak the mind of God to his people and who could unfold his will in the way that the rain brings forth life from the earth. He had a special relationship with those who were open to the Spirit and who were willing to pray in their struggle to make sense of life. He never told people what to do or how to do it. He filled them with a desire for love, joy, peace, patience and self-control. He held up the gospel as a mirror for each of us to look into our own lives.

Somehow it is a prophetic task to draw people to look at themselves differently. Like Abraham, we are called out from where we were comfortable, secure and certain of our place. We often try to go upon the journey of faith without moving from where we are. To be transformed we need to discover or create the sacred space. This can happen in the secular world. A number of modern films that have become box office successes, such as *Gandhi* have drawn me into deep reflection. Somewhere deep within I suspect that I touched freedom. People who are full of passion and can create the poetry or song that explores the human condition are a kind of revelation. Occasionally I am drawn to the idea that reality is totally different from the way it first appears. It is then that God is manifest. It is then that life had meaning. One has the feeling that the real question is being asked. Only then does one find the satisfactory answer. One realises that of those who have lost touch with the Church, many are beginning to discover that agnosticism is only part of their journey. Yet though they don't seem to miss God religious values are often still active within their moral context. If today one is to start talking to people about God one has to first touch them at the level of humanity – about what they experience in privileged moments of honesty and depth. What are the questions that make them see themselves, the world and religion differently?

The 'few words' from the pulpit on a Sunday have to be spoken in a radically transformed context. The world is totally different. We know that false softness does not heal or help. Yet the modern mentality particularly in women today rejects power and control as bad. So how do we help people to accept a nurturing authority or the challenging prophet? How do we know what we are about as priests? Do we know what is good in our religion? Can it be expressed without appearing to tell others what to do with their lives? How is it possible to protect the right to choose? How do we challenge people to accept that the good is always beyond the private ego? How can we be gospel-focused persons and avoid preaching the gospel merely as argument to support fringe questions of morality? There is little credibility in a self-righteous pulpit. Our focus can often lack breadth. We can distract from the gospel by concentrating upon the boundary issues like crime, condoms and divorce. Human feeling is not weakness and yet there is more to life. The task of bridge-building to God's truth from our own truth is a delicate mission. The primary task of the homilist is to be a prophet. He needs to 'read the signs of the times' and be a sign towards the Kingdom.

'The mysteries of faith and the guiding principles of the Christian life are expounded' in the homily.[2] 'The homily is a powerful and most suitable means of evangelisation.'[3] 'The people of God are formed into one in the first place by the word of the living God. This is quite rightly sought from the mouths of priests ... it is the first task of priests to preach the gospel ... The priests' preaching, often very difficult in present day conditions, if it is to be effective in moving the minds of its hearers, must expound the word of God not merely in a general and abstract way but by the application of the eternal truth of the gospel to the concrete circumstances of life.'[4] 'The homily is part of the liturgy.'[5] 'Pastors should carefully teach the faithful to participate in the whole Mass showing the close connection between the liturgy of the word and the celebration of the Lord's Supper, so that they can see clearly how the two constitute a single act of worship.'[6] 'It is strongly recommended that, if a sufficient number of people are present, there be a homily at week-day masses also, especially during Advent and Lent or on a feast day or on an occasion of grief.'[7]

The general instruction on the Roman Missal (26 March 1970) reminds us that the Second Vatican Council had insisted on the implementation of decisions of the Council of Trent which had been neglected. 'Among these are the homily, which must be delivered on Sundays and holydays.'[8] In all post-conciliar documents on the liturgy there is great emphasis on the importance of the homily. Both the Code of Canon Law and the Constitution on the Liturgy say that it cannot be omitted without a grave reason. There is also a realisation that the homily does not stand alone. It is important that in preparing a homily we take into account the season or feast which we celebrate. During Advent and Lent the Church asks people of faith to reflect upon their lives. In the season of Pentecost, we examine what it means to be God's people; the body of Christ; a Christian community. The theme of the individual liturgy is also important. At the Sunday liturgy the Old Testament reading and the gospel suggest this theme.

When it comes to preaching there are many other factors influencing the preparation of the priest. The word spoken is meant to call forth a response in the hearing. The Samaritan woman having heard Jesus recognised who he was. She went to town to bring her friends to Jesus.[9] After the homily we recite the creed. Our lives often declare that in spite of this verbal assent of faith we actually withhold it. In other words much preaching falls on deaf ears. Every priest knows that his congregation are in a trance or bored, that they regard his words as irrelevant or resent what he says. Some of this comes about because of the way we priests and people come to liturgy. While conviction is communication yet we must know those to whom the message is being transmitted. If we are to help people to identify God's presence in their pain or pleasure, we must heed their questions but must help them to have the right questions. We need to let them know that God's grace cannot be contained within the framework of human thinking. We cannot mark the boundaries within which we think God ought to behave.

'God does not see as man sees, man looks at appearances, but the Lord looks at the heart.'[10] This word of Samuel when choosing David underlines the wisdom needed to know the heart of those to whom we preach.

The story of David if it were contemporary would surely catch the news headlines This prophet-king whose heart God knew and who wrote some of the greatest prayers in history, (the psalms) would have had to flee in disgrace from today's media. His affair with Bathsheba the mother of Solomon would have been grist for the tabloids for years.[11] The Bible is a story of humanity and its relationship with God. A story catches the attention of everyone young and old. The Bible introduces us to a rich diversity of people all of whom relate to God in a different way. The story for example of Peter or David or Samuel or Sarah or Abraham tell us much of their humanity. It is significant that it is in their humanity rather than their sanctity that we see God at work. This, too, is significant for the homilist.

Eltin Griffin O. Carm. says that preaching is a form of contemplation.[12] He says that all true preaching is born out of Lectio Divina. First we listen to the word of God; then through repetition we receive it into the mind; then in reflection we treasure it in the heart, pondering as Mary did; and then we transpose it into life. If our homilies are to bring people to the point of assent to faith then they will need to be taught some elements of contemplation. Preaching to a congregation that is not somehow prepared to hear is futile. Some human circumstances like death or bereavement a family or parish festival or a major Church feast bring people to the liturgy with open hearts. These are powerful occasions for evangelisation.

In a world where externals, the sensational and the material predominate, prophecy is a fundamental necessity in the mission of the priest. The more we draw people towards life in the spirit or to think about life and its meaning the more they are prepared to receive the word in good soil. Those who live just for today are ill-equipped for the fruitful celebration of liturgy. In our parish we regard all the other aspects of our pastoral programme as essential to preaching. We regard proclamation as essential to the pastoral programme. Each day our daily mass begins with an introduction to the meaning of the scripture readings; the message is applied to the current concerns in the parish especially through the prayers of the faithful. Our Sunday liturgy linked to our pastoral events makes the homily the key to parish unity. With the attentiveness and the participation of those present there is a great sense of belonging and family. For others who are merely in Church by routine or habit there is little contact with the God who calls them out and there is no movement or mission. The most effective transmitter in the world can not bring its richest symphony through a radio that is not switched on. On the other hand how do we communicate with those who are switched on but are not where the message is being transmitted?

III
SHARING CHRIST'S PRIESTHOOD

Who is ready to hear the Gospel? The roots of our anger and resentment, of our lack of forgiveness, of our hardheartedness are encrusted with layers of protection. However, within us there is also a hunger for the spiritual journey – the desire for significance and meaning, the urge to touch mystery. Again we are still affected by old wounds and deep hurts. There is no other explanation for reactions that seem inappropriate to the trivial nature of the trigger.

It is something apparently simple that prevents people from

coming to Church. There is even a sense among some of them that they are better off not coming to Church at all – because they leave it angry, frustrated, disillusioned or just plain bored. They feel that they get more spiritual nourishment elsewhere. They feel it is wrong for the rest of us to assume that they are not in touch with God. They meet Christ in the poor and the needy and feel confirmed in this vision by what they hear when they pray the scriptures. Many people feel the presence of God in the depth of their being. Faith in and love of God is born in a diversity of ways.

The greatest challenge facing a parish priest today is to draw people of faith, hope, love, prayer and contemplation into the unity of one worshipping community. To convince many individuals even of goodwill that it is as a people we are to be saved is getting more difficult. That the resurrection is an invitation to us to come together to celebrate being members of Christ's risen body is not universally accepted by many modern Catholics. The notion of communion has little relevance to their daily thinking and action. In Ireland in particular the desire for a short mass underlines a great lack of understanding of the significance and centrality of liturgy for a genuine Catholic life. With so little appreciation of the spiritual riches of conscious participation in the liturgical contact with God there is little real desire for the glory of heaven. With such an attitude, the beatific magnificence of eternal life and love with God, is reduced to an eternity of the more pleasant aspects of life on earth. Evangelisation involves a new concentration on our shared 'holy priesthood' and our membership of a 'spiritual house'.

It is profitable for each of us to reflect upon what the Church obliges the 'sacred pastors' to do. They are 'obliged to fulfil each with care their task of teaching, sanctifying, and nourishing the people of God'.[13] The people of God themselves, 'by regeneration and the anointing of the Holy Spirit are consecrated to be a spiritual house and a holy priesthood'.[14] The people of God 'exercise that priesthood by the reception of the sacraments, prayer and thanksgiving, the witness of a holy life, abnegation and acts of charity, and by participation in the offering of the eucharistic sacrifice.'[15]

'The holy people of God shares also in Christ's prophetic office.'[16] What then is the specific role of the priest? While the ministerial priesthood and the common priesthood of the faithful share in the one priesthood of Christ 'they differ essentially and not only in degree'.[17] The dogmatic constitution of the Church stresses the noble vocation of the baptised. It gives a special role to the ministerial priest. By the sacred power that he has he forms and rules the priestly people; and in the person of Christ he effects the eucharistic sacrifice and offers it to God in the name of all the people.

The Church stresses the difference in essence between the ministerial priesthood and the common priesthood of the faithful. However, have we put sufficient emphasis on the fact that there is only one priesthood – the priesthood of Christ? If we helped people to understand that Christ is the priest through whom we celebrate mass and the sacraments, would they try to go it alone? If they realised for example that it is the Holy Spirit of God who forgives sin or by whose power our gifts of bread and wine become the body and blood of Christ, would they become more interested in what it means for them to be Church?[18]

How sound our vision of priesthood would become if all of us were more aware of the authority of the Holy Spirit's guidance in the whole Church. The Bible is full of people whose lives are guided by the Holy Spirit. He himself is lead by the Spirit. In the Acts of the Apostles we see that everything that happens to Jesus in the gospel happened to the Church from its founding in Jerusalem to its establishment in Rome, the centre of the world. All is the work of the Holy Spirit. Cardinal Carlos Martini, who brought the meeting at Emmaus to life in a booklet, *Praying with St Luke*, provides inspiring meditations on leadership for the parish priest.

The Latin-American priests at their general conference in

Puebla in Mexico in 1979 declared that 'the great ministry of service that the Church offers to the world and human beings in it, is evangelisation, which is offered in words and deeds'. (DV: 2) They noted that 'from the very beginning there were different ministries in the Church for the work of evangelisation. The New Testament writings depict the vitality of the Church, finding expression in many types of service. St Paul mentions the following among others: prophecy, ministry, teaching, exhortation, almsgiving, ruling and works of mercy (Rom. 12: 6-8). In other contexts Paul talks about other ministries: wisdom in discourse, discernment of spirits, and so forth (1 Cor. 12: 8-11; Eph. 4:1 1-12; 1 Thess. 5: 12ff; Phil 1: 1). Various ministries are also described in other New Testament writings.

'The divinely established ecclesiastical ministry is exercised on different levels by those who from antiquity have been called bishops, priests and deacons (LG: 28). They constitute the hierarchical ministry, which they receive in the sacrament of orders "the laying on of hands". As Vatican II teaches, through the sacrament of orders – episcopal and priestly – there is conferred a ministerial priesthood that is essentially distinct from the common priesthood shared by all the faithful through the sacrament of baptism (LG:10). Those who receive the hierarchical ministry are made "pastors" in the Church "in accordance with their function". Like the Good Shepherd (John 10:1-16), they go before the flock; they give their lives so that the flock may have life and have it in abundance; they know their flock and are known by them in turn. "Going before the flock", means being alert to the paths that the faithful are travelling so that they, united in the Spirit, may bear witness to the life, suffering, death and resurrection of Jesus Christ. Jesus, poor among the poor, announced that we all are children of the same Father and hence brothers and sisters. "Giving their lives" is the gauge of "hierarchical ministry" and the proof of greater love. That is how Paul lived, dying daily to carry out his ministry (2 Cor. 4: 11).'[19]

Much of the Puebla material is relevant to every Church striving to be transformed by the insights of Vatican II. In implementing a renewed pastoral vision there is much guidance for a parish priest. The priest is reminded of the sacrificial nature of his own loving service to the people: 'Knowing their flock and being known by them does not simply mean knowing the needs of the faithful. It means investing one's own being in them and loving as one who came to serve rather than be served (Matt. 20: 25-28).'

They re-emphasised that the priest is a man of God. He can be a prophet only insofar as he has had experience of the living God. Only this experience will make him the bearer of the powerful word that can transform the personal and social life of human beings to conform with the father's plan. Prayer in all its forms – especially the canonical hours of the breviary assigned to him by the Church – will help him to maintain this experience of God that he is supposed to share with his brothers and sisters. Like the bishop and in communion with him the priest evangelises, celebrates the holy sacrifice, and serves unity. 'As a pastor committed to the integral liberation of the poor and the oppressed the priest always operates with evangelical criteria (EN: 18). He believes in the force of the Spirit so as not to fall into the temptation of becoming a political leader, social director, or functionary of some temporal authority. For that would prevent him from being a sign and factor of unity and fraternity.'

Among priests we want to single out the figure of the parish priest. 'He is like a pastor in the likeness of Christ. He is a promoter of communion with God, his fellow humans to whose service he dedicates himself and his fellow priests joined around their common bishop. He is the leader and guide of the communities, alert to discern the signs of the times along with his people.' He encourages experiments to develop the pastoral activity of all the parish agents. 'We must support the vocational pastoral effort of ordained ministers, lay services and the religious life. Worthy of special recognition and a word of encouragement are priests and other pastoral agents.' Is not all of this equally applicable in Ireland? A return to clericalism and legalism or persevering with institutions enshrining that mentality is not God's will. Genuine pastoral care and fidelity to Christ our priest and only mediator with the father demands their total elimination from the Church.

IV
PLANNING PASTORAL COLLABORATION

Much material for a pastoral plan already exists but the leadership required to produce it is in short supply because of the changing role of the priest. 'Because pastors themselves are so actively and vitally involved in the process of the development of their role,' the US bishops committee on priestly life and ministry invited priests to 'prolong and deepen their reflections'. In a document called *A Shepherd's Care* they dealt with three areas of a pastor's ministry: spiritual, community and administrative.[20] It was their conviction 'that some of the most important issues have not yet been explored'. In the study pastors were invited to explore the religious, symbolic and spiritual significance of their role, so as to 'write a new and profound prologue to the ministry of the future'.

The priest's position in a changing environment that implies different relationships and may call for a new form of priesthood, is a major concern of the NCPI. At its annual conference in 1978 this elected body acknowledged that 'the involvement of the laity is too slow, at parish, diocesan and national level in spite of Vatican II and the Mulranny guidelines of 1974.[21] The laity commission planned a laity week for the autumn of 1980. The NCPI conference held in May 1980 urged all the priests of Ireland to give it active support. This support by their official representatives was very encouraging to priests and laity at parish level.

The conference strongly urged that structures be established for immediate dialogue to enable the laity to participate in the life of the Church. They were not speaking merely of advisory roles; they were concerned about the general non-existence of parish pastoral councils. The specifics of the setting-up of these ancillaries to the apostolic work of the Church were dealt with more than twenty-five years ago at a meeting on 9 January 1969 of sixty priests from nine dioceses at St Patrick's College, Thurles. The view then was that each local Church should 'devise its own ways and means of integrating the laity into parochial planning and decision-making'. It was acknowledged by Archbishop Morris that 'the style and dynamics must honour the existing sociology of a given community'. It was agreed that its organised Christian endeavour 'should reach beyond' ecclesiastical affairs to all the felt needs of the community.[22]

By 1980 it was acknowledged that 'today's priest needs to be much less a controller and much more an animator'. Events in Britain were also having an influence in Ireland. In that year a national pastoral conference of the Church in England and Wales was held in Liverpool. It was a gathering of lay people, religious, priests and bishops. Robert Nowell, a well-known journalist, wrote in October in the *Furrow*: 'It was not simply an exercise in consulting the faithful It was an exercise in involving them fully in the life of the Church.' The two thousand delegates at Liverpool 'were aroused to an awareness' that the Church was their responsibility. Making 'the business of being a Catholic much more challenging, much more demanding and much more costly.' It was in that context that the meeting at Emmaus took place in 1984 (*See Appendix 2*).

The re-installation of the authoritarian legalistic style of Church with the publishing of the new Code of Canon Law in 1983 has interrupted the momentum towards effective pastoral planning. The resulting docility has stifled local pastoral initiatives. People now tend again to await the lead of the bishops. The only pastoral document issued by the Irish Church since 1980 came from the Emmaus meeting at which the laity worked collaboratively with the bishops. They also used material produced by the NCPI and the Conference of Major Religious Superiors. All subsequent statements and documents issued by the hierarchy were merely of the teaching variety. The desirable collaborative processes of the 1960s and 1970s are now perceived as having been discarded. Authoritativeness is again the exclusive right of the highest clerical authority.

Meanwhile, the majority of thinking people in Ireland have moved beyond the first four stages of moral and faith development.[23] At a time when an authoritarian style has become less and less appropriate it is unfortunate that the Church has returned to this model as if it were an article of faith. Subservient pastors, the inevitable product of authoritarianism, are incapable of initiative or imaginative creativity. The young Church (Chapter 4), the Ryan report or the Emmaus document can not justly be interpreted with such an attitude. The most excellent of liturgies, the best structures require vision if renewal is to happen. The spirituality of the popular film *The Nun's Story* (1959) is still very much alive. We still value the supremacy of authority in the pilgrimage of faith. A process of shared responsibility especially at the higher levels is necessary for the new approach.

Collaboration such as happened in Liverpool and Emmaus ought to be an annual feature of Church life. If the June meeting of the hierarchy had representatives of laity, religious and priests then similar representation at diocesan and parish level would be feasible. Is it true that the human and spiritual insights of the excluded categories are of less value than those of bishops? Is it God's will that those in authority who think that all learning systems are identical should impose theirs as infallible? When we disagree with someone else are we searching for truth or merely protecting our own prejudices. How can we be sure that conflicts arise from the other person's disobedience, ignorance or egotism rather than from our own fears, lack of self-awareness or desire to be in control?

Another act which would surely symbolise the changing role of authority would be to close the national seminary at Maynooth. A commitment by the bishops to the seminaries seen as collaborative, such as All Hallows or St Patrick's in Carlow would be a significant indication of a move to equality of dignity, diversity of ministry and an end to clericalism, legalism and authoritarianism.

The parish priest does not live in isolation. He has responsibilities as a leader of the flock entrusted to his care. He has obligations to them and with them in the context of the Church universal. This dual responsibility must inform his whole life and sometimes he may feel that he is the cutting edge rather than the connecting bridge but he may not abdicate his duty to help renew Church structures. These matters are dealt with insightfully in the Ryan report.[24]

The priest's first responsibility is to the gospel; it is the leaven for Church renewal. St John, having dealt with our need for celebration in the Book of Signs (1: 2) goes on to our desire for love (13: 20). This deepest of human desires is fulfilled by Jesus. John's message is about our personal relationship with Jesus and it is more important than any office. The beloved disciple of John's gospel is loved more than St Peter, the one who held office. In his gospel all disciples are equal and the women have the same role as men. In chapter 11 Martha utters the same words of faith as Peter did and it is Mary who gives the Easter proclamation. In Luke there are eight episodes, exclusive to his work, that deal with women and Jesus's relations with them.

In our role as parish priests what do we love? What are the implications for us when we see the priority given by John to love over office or the parity given to women in Luke? Our life ceases to be a matter of saying mass and administering the sacraments. When we move into the area of pastoral planning we are challenged to change accepted structures. Praying the scriptures invites us to approach this duty with love.

V
IN LOYALTY TO PERSONS

Every Christian knows the words, 'By their fruits shall you know them' (Cf. Eph. 2: 10; Jas. 2: 26). People guided by the Spirit are recognisable by his fruits in their lives. These works are communion, participation, solidarity, love, joy, hope, peace, patience, justice achieved in self-control, unselfish giving of self, goodness – in brief, all that creates a healthy human environment. This is what points us on the way to holiness. The witness given by human beings is not based upon their own capacity but upon their confidence in the power of God.

It is my prayer that this book speaks of a new understanding of Church to those who reject authoritarianism, legalism, clericalism and triumphalism. I hope that I have encouraged the spark of trust that will enable people to venture past anger and pain to find where the fruits of the Spirit in their lives converge with the works of other Christians guided by the same Spirit. The Church is not merely an institution; it is a community of humans elevated by baptism to enable them to enter a divine community. It exists in the name of the holy trinity and has incorporated in it all those incorporated through Christ's redemptive sharing in our nature (Cf. Gal. 3: 25; 1 Cor. 2: 12; Rom. 12: 2 and 7: 6). Christ's gift of the Church to us is a pearl of great price. It is unique on earth but there were and are disturbing aspects and the Holy Spirit established in Vatican II a means for reforming these.

The theme of Vatican II was renewal which involves self-examination and an awareness of the environment. The idea implies innovation and jettisoning. Some make experiments; others look to the brakes. In true renewal there is a place for these two tendencies with the Christian spirit present to hold both on course in faith, hope and love. Understanding is the shortest distance between two points of view. This combined presence of change and conservation inevitably led to tension. A static outlook prevailed with some confusion and disagreement, not for the first time in the history of the Church. It happened in the very beginning and as a result we have guidelines. In 1 John 4: 1 we read: 'It is not every Spirit that we can trust; test then to see if they come from God.' St Paul too spoke of the need to sift the claims of those who say that they are led by the Spirit.

Renewal has take place in the liturgy, in lay organisations and in the religious orders. It is happening at diocesan level too, if less dramatically. The laity are required to manifest no less zeal. The decree on the Apostolate of the Laity requires that their commitment be broadened and intensified. It was the awareness of deep and rapid change in society that was the occasion of John XXIII's calling the Council together. His speech at its opening described difficulties which still obtain. 'Today the Church is witnessing a crisis under way within society. While humanity is on the edge of a new era, tasks of immense gravity and amplitude await the Church, as in the most tragic periods of its history. It is a question, in fact, of bringing the "modern" world into contact with the vivifying and perennial energies of the gospel, a world which exhalts itself with its conquests in the technical and scientific fields but which brings also the consequences of a temporal order which some have wished to reorganise excluding God. That is why "modern" society is earmarked by a great material progress to which there is not a corresponding advance in the moral field'.[25]

Vatican II demanded identification with the joys and suffering of the world. 'Withdrawal' spirituality, the ascetical theology of the seminary, is therefore unsuitable for the parish priest. All life, including the spiritual has to be lived. We die and rise in Christ, sharing the paschal mystery in the interaction of prayer and life and not in pious sentiment. Spirituality enlightens the quest for the deeper meaning of human existence and changes the cry for freedom from angry protest to a search for life in harmonious community. The priest is a member of that community. He is touched by God when he proclaims the word, when he presides at the liturgy. He serves Christ when he serves his fellow humans and weak vessel that he is he knows that the power which makes him spiritually effective comes from God (Cf. 2 Cor. 4: 7–11). When we move from the darkness of sin to the light and warmth of God's life we do it in the experience of daily living.

Being in touch with the ethos of his own community the priest realises that 'an authoritarianism which was accepted in the past is out of place today.'[26] At the national conference in 1987 the priests pointed out to the appropriate Vatican congregations that it 'would be a lesser love for the Church to remain silent about our need for the Church to be rooted in leadership in its local community and not seek together a better way forward.' I agree; I strive to put that vision into practice. On close examination you will most probably discover that it is the pastoral policy in your own parish.

If you have doubts about whether a collaborative style of Church is respectable read *Towards a Civilisation of Love* in which Cardinal Hume explores 'being Church' in today's world.[27] With pastoral wisdom, theological expertise and an awareness of tradition he examines different aspects of ministry in the fellowship of the people of God. He illuminates, 'how in a world addicted to power, aggression and domination [the Church] stands for unconditional love and service of others ... When society has turned its back in general on religious belief and practice the Church more than ever turns to the deepest mysteries and leads all its members into an exploration of God.'

If you are still a searcher, unsure of the relevance of these deep mysteries or of the claims of Christianity, read *Free to Believe* by Michael Paul Gallagher.[28] In little over a hundred pages it explores ten steps to faith. It helps us to get free in four 'escapes': from imprisonment in negative attitudes; from a superficial context to live differently in an alternative lifestyle, from thinking of God 'out there' to reverence the mystery within and from childish images of God to the one who is truly revealed in Jesus. The author helps us in a four-fold quest for focus: in the *heart* that hungers, in the *mind* that seeks meaning, in *conscience* awakened and in the *inner spirit* which, experiencing something of its own depths, learns to hear God's word.

Who has the courage for adventure? Why not with admission of your poverty and powerlessness come to the source from which everything springs? The freedom to love can be found even if beyond your 'place in the system', even if beyond reason. The community of the friends of Jesus at heart provides that freedom.[29] Stay with the Church in all its diversity and there you will find the one, holy, Catholic and apostolic Church; and when you have found it proclaim it from the rooftops.

1   All quotations from NCPI proceedings are taken from my own notes.
2   *Verba Dei* (21 Jan 1981). Introduction to the Lectionary.
3   *Evangelii Nuntiandi* (8 Dec 1975).
4   Decree on the Ministry/Life of the priest.
5   General instruction on the Roman Missal (26 March 1970).
6   Instruction on the Worship of the Eucharistic Mysteries (25 May 1967). For this and the other references see *Vatican II Conciliar and Post-Conciliar Documents*, Ed. Austin Flannery OP, Dominican Publications.
7   Canon 767, Code of Canon Law (1983).
8   Decree on the Ministry/Life of the priest.
9   2 Sam. 12: 7.
10   1 Sam. 16: 7.
11   2 Sam. 11, 12.
12   Speaking at the NCPI course at Guirt Muire (1988).
13   Paul VI, *Ecclesiae Sanctae* (6 August 1966).
14   *Dogmatic Constitution on the Church* (21 November 1964).
15   *Ibid*.
16   *Ibid*.
17   *Ibid*.
18   Eucharistic Prayer, 3, *Roman Missal*.
19   *Conclusions of Third General Conference of Latin-American Bishops*, National Conference of Catholic Bishops, Washington (January 1980).
20   Study published by US Catholic Conference, 1312 Massachusetts Avenue, NW, Washington DC (1984).
21   Produced after a week-long pastoral meeting of Irish bishops at Mulranny in 1974.
22   *Doctrine and Life*, Vol XIX, 1969.
23   See Chapter 1.
24   *Personal and Systemic Renewal in the Church*, NCPI, Dominic Street, Dublin.
25   John XXIII, *Humanae Salutis* (25 December1961), *Documents of Vatican II*, Geoffrey Chapman, London.
26   Statement on the appointment of bishops approved at the AGM of the NCPI (1987).
27   B. Hume, Hodder & Stoughton, London. See also *Searching for God* and

To Be a Pilgrim by the same author.

28 Darton, Longman & Todd, London. See also M. P. Gallagher, *Help My Unbelief*, Veritas/Fowler Wright.

29 Cf. Report of the sub-committee on the Systematic Theology of the Priesthood, Committee on Priestly Life and Ministry, National Conference of Catholic Bishops, Washington.

EPILOGUE

I came back to Ireland on holidays from the National College for Training Youth Leaders in Leicester at Christmas 1966. I attended a funeral at which many priests were present. Every one of them seemed angry at a report that a priest-editor of a famous English Catholic magazine had said that the Church was corrupt. There was outrage.

I had read the article. To me it was saying that, important though personal renewal was, it was not enough. Though the Church is guided by the Spirit and is the body of Christ it also has elements contributed by human weakness. These elements find expression in Church structure and policy. That Christmas I felt alone. I felt totally an outsider in this body of men in whose midst I stood. The deeply threatening question attacking me was: 'Do I really belong in the priesthood?'

I told the late Bishop Birch of this great sense of isolation. 'It takes people a long time to come to understanding,' he said. 'The notion that the Church is perfect borders upon triumphalism.' He described how he and the then Bishop of Limerick had sat on a seat in the garden of the Irish College in Rome each evening during Vatican II. They agreed to try to apply the ideas of the Council to the situation back home. They knew that it would not be 'all plain sailing'.

When brother priests, many excellent men, began to leave the priesthood I realised that acceptance and understanding were not just matters of the greatest importance for the individual; they were also vital for the future of the Church. Where the freedom to be whole, creative and committed is absent we either settle for a clericalist conformity or quit. Bishop Birch brought me beyond such drastic alternatives. Many of his contemporaries who were at the Council provided the same crucial service for their priests around the globe. They also guided us to an understanding of Church and ministry more appropriate to the pastoral insights of that magnificent Council.

It is now our turn in this generation of parish priests to understand when our parishioners feel alone in the face of an excluding legalism and clericalism. Sometimes we are accused of living in the past for promoting the ideas of a Church Council that happened thirty years ago. I feel we are living in a future that is still waiting to happen. The failures of the Council are like the failures in Christianity itself, more beloved as a theory than as a plan of action or a mission to be accomplished.

On 22 May 1993 there was a day of dialogue between women and priests from the east region of the NCPI at Tallaght, County Dublin. The issue was power and powerlessness in the Church in Ireland today. There was a role-play session where the women became priests and the priests women. The women sympathised with, and were surprised to discover the power-lessness, loneliness and isolation of, priests within Church structures. The priests did not as easily feel the powerlessness of the women. Nevertheless the dialogue produced some resolutions for the September AGM of the NCPI. At that meeting the NCPI recognised the powerlessness experienced by women within Church structures and committed itself to work for change. The east region proposed successfully a re-solution strongly supporting the further development of collaborative ministry with both men and women.The most radical aspect was the favouring of lay people's inclusion 'in the decision-making process of the Church, at local, deanery and diocesan levels'. The east region proposed that the NCPI make the following statement:

The NCPI acknowledges the powerlessness felt by priests in this era and, while this powerlessness is of a different order to that experienced by woman in the Church, it is nonetheless experienced as real.

A continuation of this dialogue took place on 26 March 1994.

For many the accepted ways of looking at things no longer make sense taking account of their experience of life and their stage of moral development. They are as explorers of a new continent where they will find the same Jesus Christ in all his riches. He shows them that they are to live as his people in community and free participation. By praying the scriptures we are freed to see the stages of our growth from a religion of fear or rewards to one of acceptance of its innate truthfulness and goodness. The resolutions adopted by the NCPI are necessary to transport us to this new continent. Otherwise the frustration, isolation, cynicism and lack of direction, addressed by the NCPI resolution, will intensify.

There is a widespread belief that the bishops guard the gate to the new continent. Surely this is only true if we accept a single model of Church – the model rejected by the Council. Yet when people who believe in action get moving at parish level they discover that there are no walls round the new continent. There is no gate to guard. Those whose knowledge is merely academic lack wisdom; those who experience Church discover:

1 that life is not meaningless and God is a not a hoax
2 that the most desired values of human life – love, unconditional acceptance, belonging, a blending of learning and experience, youth and age, forgiveness and reconciliation – are also the ingredients of a Christian family and the creators of a healthy human environment
3 that prayer in such a context draws us into a family of families building a society of justice, experience and responsibility
4 that authoritativeness comes from the experience of a life lived caringly and responsively, bypassing the narrow focus of legalism and authoritarianism
5 that no one ever has the whole truth or the fulness of love because these are divine attributes
6 that a parish that helps people find meaning in their lives, giving them a sense of dignity and belonging in a caring

Christian community which answers their religious needs best facilitates the proclamation of the gospel. Is not this the Church in miniature?

There are additional bonuses for parochial clergy. The pain or anger we feel at the sterile, platitudinous support of official Church documents diminishes. When we know that there is only one master, the real significance of authority in our lives is discerned. Willingness to take our own initiatives replaces disillusionment at lack of leadership in an authoritarian structure. Our interior freedom makes legalism irrelevant, the sharing of ministry breaks down clericalism. Living in the parish as family is an antidote to loneliness and isolation. Community support helps us realise that media preoccupations need not demoralise it. Contact with the humanity of the bishop unveils his Christian and pastoral concern bonding us as a diocesan family.

Seeing how God interacts with people in their lives brings us all beyond aimlessness and brokenness. This parish has experienced the death of ten children, four teenagers and three young fathers in five years. In that hurricane of grief the healing presence of Christ was amply evident. It helped us to be a community of dialogue and decision, of petition and prayer. Together we have journeyed through the desert drawn by compassion and guided by the scriptures and prayer. We have our own Solomons, Jobs, Davids and Hoseas. We have seen Elizabeth and Mary, Simeon and Zachariah, several apostles and a great diversity of saints.

In facing the unpalatable in our lives we meet Jesus the high priest. Feeling forsaken by his father and alone on the cross, he in his perfect sacrifice of self established his right relation between God and humans. His work done for all is perpetually effective (Heb. 7: 27). This Jesus whom the Church serves is transcendent, greater than the world, greater than the Church. Authority there is not self-generated; Christians live from a source different from ourselves. We confess that grace and authority are gifts of him who is obedient to the father. Our obedience through the Church transcends legalism and author-itarianism. Our ministry as priests is not given by the comm-unity but discerned there. The prayerful wisdom of the people coupled with that of the bishop (or others entrusted with authority) incorporates this ministry into its life and mission. Since God calls us as a people then it is as a people that we ought to discern, call empower and send the gifted into God's vineyard. The harvest is great ... the fields are ripe.

In the appendices which follow, particularly in Appendices 6 and 7, we provide a map for a journey. We invite you to set out, slowly this time, as you re-read the story of our journey. You will note how we *must* set out anew each day in regard to some aspect because there is so much failure. It is our nature. You will find that you are on a similar journey and that it is good for us to be here. May we be together with all our diversity and may the Lord be with us.

APPENDIX 1

A COMMUNIST THREAT OR A STRUGGLE FOR JUSTICE?

'As an act of expiation, and to invoke the Divine Aid and the blessing of peace, we hereby direct that a Triduum of Prayer be opened in every Parish Church and in all Religious Houses on Tuesday, 3 November, in preparation for the Feast of All the Irish Saints; the devotions to consist of the Rosary and the Litany of the Irish Saints, in the presence of the Blessed Sacrament exposed. We call upon our people to join in these devotions with the utmost zeal and fervour. The Religious behind their Convent walls will, we know give Ireland, in her hour of trial, the benefit of their prayers. And we expect all our teachers to urge the children under their care, both boys and girls, to join in the crusade of prayer. Finally, we direct our priests to exert every effort to keep young people from secret societies, and diligently instruct them on the malice of murder, and the satanic tendencies of Communism.[1]

Thus ended a pastoral letter issued from the annual October meeting of the Irish bishops in 1931. The bishops were concerned at attempts to 'mobilise the workers and working farmers of Ireland behind a revolutionary movement to set up a Communistic State'. They saw the entrance of communism to Ireland 'disguised for the moment in terms of Nationality and zeal for Farmers and Workmen, but which are to serve as revolutionary units to infect their disciples with the virus of communism and create social disruption by organised opposition to the law of the land.'

The 'Catholic Hierarchy's momentous pronouncement' was the full page headline in the *Kilkenny People*. It gave the full text of the bishops' 'condemnation of communistic propaganda'.

The names and dioceses of the four archbishops, and twenty-four bishops, who signed the letter are printed in full. There was 'grave anxiety' lest the 'blasphemous denial of God, the overthrow of Christian civilisation, class warfare, the abolition of private property and the destruction of family life' was about to occur in Ireland. The bishops made it clear that they felt 'called upon' to issue the pastoral because of the religious and moral aspects of the affair.

They left the judgement on questions of public policy to the political arena. 'We cannot remain silent in the face of the growing evidence of a campaign of a revolution and communism, which if allowed to run its course unchecked must end in the ruin of Ireland both body and soul,' the bishops declared. Much of the evidence of 'the campaign of revolution and communism', came from this small rural parish. The establishment of a miners' union affiliated to the Socialist International was one of the direct links between communism and Ireland.

The early 1930s was a time of intense debate in Ireland, particularly with regard to political and social affairs. Full pages of the *Kilkenny People* and *The Post* were given to reporting these public debates. The quality was very high. The speeches showed signs of careful research. A meeting on 27 October 1932 of the Unemployed Able-Bodied Men's Association is a good example. The City Hall in Kilkenny was the venue. The issues arose from a previous meeting of the permanent and temporary employees of the county council. Patrick Walsh, its chairman, insisted that the Unemployed Able-Bodied Men's Association 'did not expound the doctrines of Lenin, Trotsky, Stalin, Louis Blanc. We are only interested in trying to promote schemes for the welfare of the unemployed,' he said. He appealed for a just share of the wealth being flaunted vulgarly in the face of hungry men and starving people. 'There is only one source of production of wealth and that is labour power,' he claimed, to loud applause.

Mr Walsh warmed to his theme that, ' God beneficently has created all things to be enjoyed in common by all living beings and that the earth is the common possession of all'. He had apt quotations from Pope Leo XIII, SS Clement, Basil the Great, Gregory Nicodemus, Ambrose, Chrysostom and others to establish that the doctrines they were expounding, doctrines by very prominent Irishmen like William Thompson, Wolfe Tone, Fintan Lalor and James Connolly, saw 'eye to eye' with popes, ancient Church fathers and modern French socialists.

A 'big meeting' on 2 October 1931 also merited a full page report in the *Kilkenny People*. 'Two bus loads brought a big contingent of men from Clogh.' The *Kilkenny People* reported that the large meeting was presided over by an active Fianna Fáil councillor and that Mr Nicholas Boran of Clogh, 'who recently visited Russia was the principal local speaker'. At the meeting Mr Boran outlined his priorities. He described confidence as the capitalist knew it, as a guarantee, 'that could give the capitalist investing money that the slaves would work without looking for better conditions and would accept exploitation. If they got that guarantee the capitalist would invest their money and if it could not be given they would not.' Nicholas Boran saw a 'wholesale attack upon wages and upon the workers to lower their conditions'. He said that international organisations were the only way to break the back of such an attack upon workers.

Dr Patrick Collier, Bishop of Ossory, wrote a pastoral letter, which was read at all the masses in the diocese on the 1 January 1933. The text almost filled a full page of the *Post*. Dr Collier said, 'There can be no doubt but that communism has touched Ireland. A few weeks ago our city and the industrial area of the county (Clogh) shared in the communistic push.'

He analysed why they had 'witnessed a considerable expansion of communism in the world. We have the symptoms of the communistic disease; those who are in a position to know, who have first hand information, tell us to beware. We in Kilkenny have reason to know how true that warning is. We have the only coal-mining area in the country employing hundreds of workers. Such a centre is always the hope of the communistic agitator.' He appealed to the leaders of labour to beware of communism. 'To those concerned, I appeal with all the strength of my heart and soul to abandon dangerous organisations which can only lead to total ruin of soul and body. This appeal I make in a very special way to those leaders and their followers who are Catholics and Irishmen. Up to this I am sure the leaders and agents themselves are led astray. They cannot understand the full implications and consequences of communism'. He then went on to 'warn all obstinate leaders or agents of communism in this diocese' that 'we will fight for our faith with the tenacity and courage of our forefathers; we will expose; we will oppose; we will win.'

The Bishop followed up this pastoral letter with a visit to Moneenroe in the parish of Clogh. There was a very emotional sermon in the Church. The workers were given the choice of standing under the red flag of communism or 'where Ireland always stood, under the standard of Christ'. Thirty-three people who did not see their membership of the miners' union as opposed to their belief in God were excommunicated that day.

The vast majority of the miners did not regard themselves as communists. Those who saw themselves as socialists as outlined by Mr Walsh at the Kilkenny meeting felt that their excommunication was an injustice imposed by the Church itself. The last miner to be reconciled with the Church did so after agreeing that his 'row' had been with Churchmen rather than with the Church.

The controversy also brought political conflict. General O'Duffy, at a United Ireland demonstration in Kilkenny reported in the *Kilkenny People* on 28 October 1933 criticised District Justice O'Shea. At the hearing of a case on 19 September 1933 he had said, 'I don't think there is any communism here at all. Except for suggestions through the press recently I never saw any sign of it. It might be suggested that the labour troubles here in Kilkenny last year were due to it. I don't believe that. I believe they were caused by ignorance, foolishness, and want of organisation on the part of some people.' This was District

Justice O'Shea's assessment. 'An attempt that barely reached the fringe of the county had been made to get people subscribe to the monstrous institution that communism is' he admitted but 'this does not justify the suggestion that there is communism here.'

Meanwhile, the previous Sunday at the close of a mission in the neighbouring Doonane parish, there was ample evidence of the clergy's conviction that the labour troubles were evidence of the real threat of communism. Father A. Hipwell, PP, who officiated at the close of the mission said it was a great consolation to him to know that every man in the parish had attended the mission and the sacraments. Father Ignatius, OFM (Cap), Kilkenny, who conducted the mission was 'more than pleased with the results of [his] labours in Doonane', because some people told him they had 'finished with communism'.

The material in the *Kilkenny People* and the *Post* from that era would make a library of books. There were many letters also to the editor, with several contributions from a Dominican priest, Fr Coleman. His letter to the *Kilkenny People* of 17 October 1931 had 3,000 words. The contribution of the clergy and bishops who were prepared to go public saw the entire question as one of a great threat of communism. The working people on the other hand saw the very same issue as one entirely about their working conditions. For them it was a matter of justice. Their conviction led them to take the parish priest down into the mines to see the atrocious circumstance of their employment. He was shocked. Yet his perspective never entered the public arena. Today we are still living with that history. We are trying to discover how a part of the question becomes the whole question, leading to a confrontational perspective.

---

1   All quotations are taken from the files of the *Kilkenny People* (1930-1933). Their kind permission to study those 300 weekly papers is deeply appreciated. A book about the period could provide many insights for this time of change, especially in the relationship between the official Church and local communities.

APPENDIX 2

There are many examples of the effectiveness of collaboration both within the Church and between the Church and civic organisations. One of the most important was a special meeting of the Irish Bishops' Conference at Emmaus Retreat Centre, Swords, on 22–27 September 1986. A four page report by Dr Joseph Cassidy, spokesman for the hierarchy, on Saturday 27 September 1986 has become known as the Emmaus document.[1]

He stressed to the media that essentially the meeting was a week of prayer and reflection on the mission of the Church. 'Its purpose was not to produce precise formulae or a set of specific decisions but to identify areas of significance.' The bishops agreed to stress at the outset that 'all of us, bishops, priests, religious and laity have, by reason of our common baptism, a shared responsibility in the life and mission of the Church. We have equality of membership but different roles; we have diversity of function, but multiplicity of gifts and each member of the Church has his or her own place which no one else can fill.'

Submissions from the NCPI, the Conference of Major Religious Superiors, other commissions of the Bishops' Conference, and lay people all over the country inspired the bishops' decisions. The involvement of eleven members of the Laity Commission was one of the most significant events in recent Church history. Areas of importance that the laity and bishops identified during that week were the parish, prayer, work and justice and the place of women and the young in the Church.

It is 'in the parish that lay people experience a sense of belonging to and a sense of participation in the life of the Church'.

So they devoted a lot of time thinking about the renewal of parish life, the building up of community, greater participation by lay people in the life of the Church at parish level. Their vision for every parish in the country was a liturgy group to assist the priest in the preparation for Sunday Mass and in the preparation of all parents prior to their children's receiving baptism, First Confession, Holy Communion and Confirmation.

Very much aware of the need that people feel for study and for a deepening of their faith, they stressed adult religious formation. They acknowledged that some very good models of parish already exist and called for every parish where pastoral councils did not exist to form one. Parish visitation by priests and ministry to special groups such as handicapped, the sick, the old, the poor and the bereaved was seen as 'an absolute priority'. Their basic principle was that every parish should be 'a place where everybody feels involved, wanted and loved'.

The second area of importance identified was that of prayer. 'There is among people, including the young, a hunger for prayer and a desire to know how to pray,' Dr Cassidy said. We see the need for a concerted effort to train people in methods of prayer'. Cardinal Martini, Archbishop of Milan made a 'major contribution', as keynote speaker. When he went to Milan, a huge industrial city with five million Catholics, he wondered, what was the first thing he should stress when he became archbishop in that enormous industrial complex. He decided that he should put the emphasis at the very beginning on prayer, on silence and on contemplation. He said he was amazed at the response. The cathedral in Milan was regularly packed with young people anxious to hear the word of God, to listen to it, to contemplate it in silence and to pray about it. So many came – they came in their thousands – that they had to disperse them in ten or twelve big Churches throughout the city. 'So, prayer has to be a priority with us,' agreed the bishops and the laity present.

They considered the young 'not in isolation, as a separate

species, but as part of a maturing Church'. Since they 'do have specific needs in the areas of liturgy, leisure, work and, tragically non-work in too many cases', the bishops' conference promised to look at the liturgy to see how it might be adapted 'to make it more relevant to the lives and concerns of young people'. One of their major concerns, in regard to youth was the high level of unemployment. They set a programme for the Church to:

a) Promote a new perception of work to include not just work for wages but also work which is a service to the community. The irreplaceable Christian witness of lay people is in their daily life at work. 'We recognise that many people are deeply influenced at work by their Christian faith, but there are many others in the world of work who tend to be influenced more by group- or self-interest rather than by Christian principles. We feel, therefore, there is need to emphasise that many of the concerns we expressed in the *Work of Justice*, our pastoral letter, are still very relevant today.[2] The work of social justice is a vital part of the gospel.'

b) Stress more and more the obligations of property, wealth and labour. 'Those who have wealth and jobs must be reminded over and over again that they have obligations towards the unemployed and deprived, and they should be encouraged to promote and help to finance local initiatives and enterprise to that end.'

c) Be sensitive herself to the social realities in a practical way by helping to provide employment, centres of information, counselling and so on. Many parishes and Church groups – this is worth emphasising because it's true – are already providing employment at local level, often in co-operation with state agencies.

d) Try to contain the evil consequences of unemployment by endeavouring to prevent human deterioration. Unemployment is the most serious problem facing society. 'It is actively destructive of personal morale, of self-worth and of the happiness of the family and of the wellbeing of society.

There is often a kind of apathy in the face of so much unemployment. People are very often totally demoralised by protracted idleness, or, more accurately, by their continued failure to find work through repeated rejection. It is very demoralising, so the Church must do what it can to prevent what we call human deterioration.'

The bishops were concerned that a number of young people, especially the urbanised young, are no longer or infrequently practising the faith. 'It does represent a serious challenge for the Church. Motivated lay people are best placed to lead them to active membership of the Church – the apostolate of laity to laity, the apostolate of youth to youth.' They called on lay people to help in that mission. In their general consultations and discussions before and during the meeting, emphasis was placed by them on the need for greater involvement of women in non-ordained ministry. The bishops recognised that need and actively desired as a conference equal representation for women and men in Church bodies at local and national level. It is very important that at these different levels the ideas, the insights and gifts of women, lay and religious are heard. Bishop Cassidy emphasised that it was a 'week without ending, because the process of consultation and decision-making and implementation will still go on'.

In the areas of education and health almost all our schools and many of our hospitals provide daily examples of the value of co-operation between Church and state. Concern for the pupil or the patient is the meeting point of that co-operation. Sometimes when there is a crisis the relationship between Church and state institutions merits more public attention. If this crisis involves a moral dimension there can also be a highly emotive interest. An example of a collaborative approach in such a crisis was the commission set up at the time of the Kilkenny incest case. The Church of Ireland and the Roman Catholic communities were jointly represented at the McGuinness inquiry by the clergy from our parish. We made the following points:

1   Crisis is the only unlocking mechanism to enter the health
    system.
    a) In social dimensions a problem has to become public.
    b) It is unable to break a downward spiral. The social
       worker was in contact with Mrs X for two years. Whose
       problem? What service is responsible?
    c) Co-operation is a theory. In practice there is hostility.
       Clergy can motivate community care. Health Board –
       give lip-service to it but have no antennae for real
       community contact. Local nurse/social worker 'carrying
       the can' without supports. Other local professionals
       such as teachers are not taken into the confidence of the
       health authorities.
2   Our attempts to engage the services:
    a) At meetings of local professionals, teachers at home/
       happy with contact while the health officials seemed
       threatened. On the ground children reject help from the
       physical and emotional distance of health board while
       teachers are daily present.
    b) Health professionals threatened by community, clash
       between their clinical legal approach and the com-
       munity's caring, let's-get-it-done approach.The health
       board sees services *for* where people feel treated as
       objects, appointments times, etc. Communities see
       services *with*, where people are treated as subjects/
       persons. Community unsupported – No psychiatric
       service for youth – Psychiatric service – pushing people
       back into community without links into that community
       and its caring dimension.
    c) Submission to Minister of Community Care re issues like
       suicides and violence. (*See Chapter 6, Section 1*)
3   Alienation:
    a) Bishop Peter Birch: 'Poor do not trust authority'. Depend
       on the Priest/Politician to unlock the system – made to
       feel inadequate. System seen as excluding agencies.
    b) State itself is regarded as more a service of injustice than

justice. High pay for assessment/diagnosis – No money for care/cure. No community care system in effect – especially in the area of support for the carers. Tax yesterday – payments months/years later.

c) The absence of trust. Do carers feel unprotected legally? Especially in the journey from symptom easily recognised by teachers for example and often by neighbours. Gardaí are seen as protected in investigating occurrences e.g., neglect, abuse etc. – But what protection has the teacher/priest/social-worker? In an alienated society gardaí and their system are not acceptable. People protect their own from the judicial process, even drug pushers, blue movie peddlers, alcoholic abusers, etc.

d) Solutions should be community based and schools are the only state agencies, which have access to parents and the voluntary community care system. The distance between the professional care service and the need adds to the alienation. Locals know better than the visitor over whose eyes it is easier to pull the wool! There is also a chronic delay between the problem and the response in service, provided from the distance.

e) Persons within these unresponsive institutions feel threatened in their professional competence by the unpalatable nature of these facts. The stronger the threat the more intense the denial.

The individual social worker is often the scapegoat for the inadequacy or unsuitability of the token service. The McGuinness inquiry proved to be a much better listener than was expected from the establishment. However its recommendations were severely handicapped by being basically a health board inquiry. An effective inquiry would have representatives from justice, education, social welfare and voluntary or Church bodies.

---

1   Statement for news conference, Catholic Press and Information Office, 27 September 1986.
2   Irish Bishops' Pastoral, *The Work of Justice*, Veritas. Cf. *Work is the Key*.

APPENDIX 3

Some people think that each parishioner is entitled to be elected to any group in the parish. We try to help people discover that the Church is made up of members with a variety of gifts. Our task is to try and match the individual gift to each particular need. We involve people in this search in a variety of ways. Initially the pastoral council sent out a double-sided inquiry sheet; one side sought the opinions of parishioners; the other side listed areas for involvement. There was a 30% response to this survey of opinion. This is the inquiry:

YOUR OPINIONS

[This headed the first page]

1) What is the best time of year for a mission?

2) What is the best time for Sunday mass?
   Moneenroe   Clogh
   What is the best time for daily mass?

3) Would you accept prayer in your home led by the priest ... parish sister ... member of Legion of Mary ... Youth Minister ... Eucharistic Minister ... Ministers of the Word ...?

4) Do you object to Church-gate collections?

5) What do you see as a priority for the parish?
   (a)
   (b)
   (c)

6) What should be happening that is not happening?
   (a)
   (b)
   (c)

7) What is the best thing about the parish?
   (a)
   (b)
   (c)

8) What is the worst thing about the parish?
   (a)
   (b)
   (c)

9) What I really want to say to the priest is:

YOUR ACTION

[This headed the reverse side]

1) Name the member of your family willing to help in the parish:

Name   Address

   (a) as Collector
   (b) as Reader
   (c) as Choir member
   (d) as Cleaner
   (e) as Offertory gift bearer
   (f) Saying prayers of faithful

2 As a member of the parish Liturgy Group co-ordinating
   above

3 Promoting or involvement through Parish Pastoral Group
   or on
   (a) St Vincent de Paul
   (b) Legion of Mary
   (c) Social Service Group
   (d) Cemetery Carers committee
   (e) Adult Religious Education
   (f) Bereavement Support

4 Helping families by active involvement in
   (a) Parenting Group
   (b) School Parents Council
   (c) School Board
   (d) Baby Sitter Club

5 Help our Young People through Parish Youth Council or
   as Adult Leader with
   (a) Youth Club Clogh or Moneenroe
   (b) Community Games
   (c) Under age hurling/football
   (d) P.T.A.A.
   (e) Camogie
   (f) Hall Development Committee
   (g) School Finance

We catch the mood to encourage involvement. To extend the
spirit of the mission we 'pushed' involvement in the liturgy.
We circulated and preached the following document:

   The Church reminds us often that we are a community who
worship – not a random collection of individuals. What really
forms us as community is taking part together in the mass –
each of us having the opportunity to perform our proper
function.

Family participation at funerals and weddings is excellent. Family preparation for sacraments is reasonably good and the extent of family involvement (with children for first confession and confirmation) in Sunday liturgy and the child's religion programme during Lent was edifying. Involvement in special liturgies, e.g, during the Christmas season, Holy Week, Corpus Christi, the annual Lourdes week and annual SVP mass is also excellent.

Now a special effort is being made to increase our desire to make our involvement in the Church each weekend as fulfilling as our involvement in the parish mission before Easter. The director of the National Liturgical Centre, Fr Paddy Jones, is coming to help us. On Wednesday 23 and Wednesday 30 October from 7.30 – 9.30 p.m. at the Railyard Clubrooms he will help us to look at 'Liturgy as Parish Life'.

Then under the leadership of the Parish Liturgy Team we will set up an action group in both Clogh and Moneenroe to set the pace for our involvement. This group will go to the Liturgy Centre at Carlow for further training. All who wish to get involved are welcome. Everyone is welcome. All are welcome.

The other side of community involvement is having masses at times to suit the people. Each person/family could nominate a time that fits in with their life pattern. Our question is not so much a question of what time our four weekend masses should be celebrated as 'What time should we have our four masses so that you will be able to celebrate the eucharist within and as part of our own community. Please talk to the other members of your household and tick off the times your family deems the most suitable (We enclosed a voting paper; it focused interest).

Missing mass: A disturbing feature of our parish life is the unwillingness of some parishioners to join us for mass. This is a serious wound in our desire to be community at worship.

The Parish Pastoral Council is anxious to hear of their reasons for not being with us. We would like to hear in particular from those who seldom go to mass at all or who come but seldom go into the Church. Tell the priests 'in strict confidence' and as a parish we will try to remove the obstacles to their being with us. It may be as simple as providing a crèche for small children or we may have to tell people the meaning and importance of our weekly gatherings as God's people.

From now until Pentecost keep praying about how we can become truly a Church by being missionary, i.e., bringing home the lukewarm, 'the lost', 'the wounded', the 'little ones'. Please play your part.

Thank you

Occasionally we deliver the following census forms to each house. This we do to assist us in filling out the 'Annual Parish Returns for the Diocese of Ossory' – a statistical and pastoral report on parish life sought by the bishop at the end of each year. This is returned on the second weekend of the New Year.

CENSUS FORM

1 Number in Household
   A Children preschool
   B Children in Primary School in Parish
   C Children in Primary School outside Parish
   D Children in Post-Primary Schools
   E Children in Third Level Education in other Education,
      e.g., FÁS course
   F Adults: 18–65 years
   G Adults: over 65 years

2 Number in Household
   (a) in full-time paid employment/self-employed
   (b) Unemployed
   (c) Who emigrated
   (d) Who took up employment anywhere in Ireland

Name of person of household who signs this form
Name   Address

Please fill out this Census Form. It is the bishop's wish that we carry out this census carefully and accurately.The period covered is Saturday 12 January and Sunday 13 January 1991.

At the end of a three-year period of striving to involve the laity and the end of term of office of most parish groups a major visitation of the parish took place. The following letter was sent out by the priests and each house was visited by the parish sisters, the deacon or the two priests.

PARISH VISITATION

This year our parish visitation takes a new form. Between now and Christmas three clergy and two sisters will between them knock at every door in the parish. We have four reasons for visiting:

(1) We would like to hear each family's need, opinion and desire for involvement.

(2) We are now at the end of a period of experimentation in involving the laity in the life of the Church. Overleaf is a list of parish organisations. When we visit you can tell us which group the members of your family are already helping with or are willing to do so.

(3) In particular we would like to hear your family's view on:
things of which you approve of in the parish;
things of which you do not approve;
things that are not happening that you would like to see happening.

(Do not forget to help make things happen: play your part by volunteering for some of the items overleaf).

(4) We would like to hear what style of mission you would like next year.

Your views will receive careful consideration. Your involvement is welcome and appreciated. If you have a special skill don't be shy about letting us know about it!

Looking forward to hearing your view sometime between now and Christmas. Thank you for the part you play in the community life of our parish. May God bless all your undertakings.

In addition to the usual survey question the following opportunities for involvement were discussed with each household. Some families had thought and talked about it; others didn't remember receiving it; yet it made the parish visitation a much more purposeful exercise for the priests especially, providing an agenda for much more constructive conversation.

It helped us to flesh out the census noting the school/ college, date of birth of the children, place of work at home/ abroad and then paternal and maternal ancestry. For our visit we had prepared a file of questions, spaced for recording the replies and suggestions from each household. We noted much goodwill and a great diversity between the concerns of the people and our vision for a Church of mission.

PARISH GROUP ORGANISATION IN WHICH YOU ARE INVOLVED OR
WISH TO BE INVOLVED:

A) Liturgy Group
   1 Liturgy Group
   2 Ministers of Eucharist
   3 Minister of Word
   4 Adult Choir
   5 Folk Choir
   6 Musician
   7 Cantor
   8 Prayers of the Faithful
   9 Offertory Gift Bearer
   10 Commentator
   11 Cleaner/Decorator
   12 Family Liturgy
   13 Usher
   14 Altar Server

B) Finance Committee
   1 Fundraising
   2 Halls/Schools
   3 Maintenance
   4 Holidays/Outings
   5 Pilgrimages
   6 Emergency Relief
   7 Colliery Dev Group
   8 Colliery Housing Group
   9 Educational Dev
   10 Administration
   11 Collector
   12 Counter

C) Social
   1 Pastoral Council
   2 Parents Council

3 Parenting Course
4 St Vincent de Paul
5 Day Care
6 Youth Ministry
7 Youth Club
8 Youth Club (Jnr)
9 Youth Dev or Faith Friends
10 Hospitality or Bereavement Support
11 Legion of Mary
12 Community Alert
13 Community Games
14 Brownies/Guides
15 Juvenile G.A.A.
16 Youth Drama/Musical
17 Other * (See below).

D) Services Requested
1 Promoting Justice
2 Human Dev Prog
3 Enneagram Course
4 Home Management
5 Rosary/Prayer Group
6 Scripture Group
7 Counselling
8 Spiritual Direction
9 Baptismal Team
10 Mission (Ecumenical)

E) Special help required if all of D) above, i.e., Baptismal/
   Marriage preparation. (Training provided to those interested in offering their service.)

---

* For example you may be already a member of ICA/Ladies Club/
   Community Council/Credit Union/GAA/Soccer/Boxing/Adult Drama.

APPENDIX 4

Effective pastoral action presupposes good management. This demands careful planning, on-going clarification and constant evaluation. Notions about the role of the priest are so deeply imbedded in lay and clerical thinking that everyone knows how the priest ought to think and act! Some of these are obstacles to an effective pastoral plan. Priests are taught to think of themselves as something they *are* rather than as people with a job to do. Laity often see the parish priest as someone with the status and power to get something done. There is also a presumption that an appointment as a parish priest bestows the ability to handle all it demands.

At the pastoral level there is little agreement about the role of priest or laity. The general notion is that the priest's job is about mass and the sacraments. If he can preach well then mass is not boring. But the parish priest is the community president. This involves the ability to manage resources and personnel. So he needs to think, understand and act as a manager. We tend to think of the priest in the way we think of those of recognised professions or vocations, specialists in their own field. But if a primary task of the parish priest is building a Christian community then the ability to work with and motivate people is essential.

The parish priest has to have a clear idea of where he stands in relation to experts and all the other people whose roles impinge on his leadership. The parish exists for people and to do things with them and for them according to the will of Christ. To avoid so much muddled thinking in pastoral matters, clear distinctions about different functions within the parish as an organisation is vital. The parish priest is the one responsible for keeping the parish as a living community working properly. This is a very active occupation. It demands a lot of thinking, decision-making, action and evaluation.

The use of a collaborative approach to the pastoral management of the parish has several advantages. Central to our attempts at more effective leadership is the constant use of the little words: what; when; who; why; how and where.[1] In replying to these we strive to be both action- and people-conscious. We consider both what has to be done to get the results we desire and who is going to do it. We deal with problems in morale, attitudes and ability. On the team we take note of what each member is capable of doing and their priorities. We strive to blend this variety of ability and priorities into a simple action plan. I see it as my role to think in terms of needs to be met, obstacles and problems to be overcome, delaying tactics that will cause tension and the sensitivities of those with different objectives or priorities.

All of the team treat the people of the parish as individuals, as families and as members of many splendid parish groups. We look at ability, attitudes and motivation from the most positive perspective and provide awareness training and formation to help cope with the negative and shadowy aspects. We strive to help people make the most productive use of their talent and time particularly in their organisation of meetings. Failure here is the most soul destroying aspect of the clericalist-hierarchical culture. Decisions are *conscious* choices. In many clericalist gatherings the assumption is that there is no decision to be made! Therefore action is never planned and so cannot happen.

I had to be weaned from that attitude because I was unconsciously bringing it to my priestly work. The most effective formation which I received for my role as parish priest occurred in secular institutions and organisations: in leadership, communication, group work, developmental social work and in research and evaluation. In establishing structures of involvement in youth work and radio and in having a particular role within these structures I learned to distinguish between the specialist things which I did myself and of the very different role of *making things happen*.

In the latter there were also long-term plans and day-to-day happenings which required on the spot decisions. Flexibility and freedom and a willingness to *accept* responsibility for the decision taken brings clarity to leadership.

Most priests can bring adequate managerial knowledge to Church structures. They will find that adequate resources are already available to them within the parish as an organisation, given the proper objectives. A major obstacle to be overcome is a conflict of priorities between those with whom they work and the dictates of the Church universal. We look on Church regulations as helpful guidelines, to be modified according to the demands of the gospel and Church teaching in our particular circumstance. We pay particular attention to feedback inviting comment on parish initiatives and on our leadership.[2]

The most important aspect of evaluation is assessment of our own leadership performance. The assistance of others is helpful, particularly when we perform as a team outside of the parish.

The following set of questions is used when that happens. When we fail to use an evaluation technique the feedback is often confined to impressions rather than reality.

(1) From our presentation, paying particular attention to the documentation we presented to the meeting, what do you see as:

    (a) the most notable characteristics of the parish.

    (b) our basic pastoral principles.

    (c) as our vision of parish.

    (d) our most successful strategies for involving laity in the life and *mission* of the Church.

(2) In the light of the parish priest's responsibility for the pastoral, spiritual and administrative leadership did you find any evidence of his:
    (a) willingness to share that leadership?
    (b) capacity and decision to share it?
    (c) opting out of that responsibility?
    (d) exercising the role in a manner that excludes the parish team or the variety of parish groups?

(3) How did you assess the team itself:
    (a) The lay leadership of the day and the linking and co-ordination of entire presentation.
    (b) the contribution of individuality and diversity to the richness of the pastoral initiatives at the level of ideas and action, mirroring the work of the Holy Spirit creating unity from diversity.
    (c) its consistency in emphasising the Church as the mission – called by God and sent by him and *not* a democracy reflecting the more personal perspectives of its members.

(4) What did you note as significant in their personal experience that helped each team member, for example:
    (a) How membership of a group, e.g., School Board, Parenting Course, Charismatic Renewal, Religious Community, led to a deeper commitment to the mission of the Church and overall pastoral dimension of the parish.
    (b) The part participation in training courses had in their *practical* contribution to Clogh and in the *evolution* of the Team itself.
    (c) How their own faith journey in its social and historical context effected their coming to involvement.
    (d) How the native-born provided enlightenment in shaping our mission to the specific circumstances of the parish and how other members could draw a community beyond its pains and prejudices.
    (e) in its role in the parish in providing formation, information and leadership to draw others into discerning individual gifts for active service in the mission of the

Church in the parish.

(5) How did the presentation help you to share and evaluate:

   (a) Your own call to be Church and its mission in the parish.

   (b) Your present contribution to parish ministry and how it might change in the future.

   (c) How you might bring the insights of your parish formation or ministry course to the service of your own parish.

   (d) Your vision of your own parish.

(6) Could you identify any happening in your life where you knew that your attitudes, feelings, ideas and behaviour all played a part in planning for a group when, how, why, where ...

   (a) Were their attitudes, flexible, rigid, spontaneous, inhibited or hostile.

   (b) Did your feelings, level of self-esteem, sense of acceptance or rejection, submission or domination, self-reliance or dependence affect the outcome in any way?

   (c) Was your behaviour supportive, critical, constructive, negative, sensitive, emotional, rational?

   (d) List the positive ideas you suggested. Who planned the *action* following and who saw it through? How was it evaluated?

Questions 1, 2, 5 and 6 should be helpful in using the book to get a picture of our parish. When we are confident in our own role and method we then begin to get out the message.

---

1   See page 43 for an explanation of our Tree of Life.
2   See Appendix 3, particularly page 185.

APPENDIX 5

Using every medium at our disposal to communicate the message is a pastoral priority. Community radio is an excellent medium for dialogue. The local papers have correspondents in each parish. They are always interested in receiving information and reports. In a survey of people's reading habits I discovered that young and old read the local notes in the paper. Very little else is read except entertainment information by the young and sport by the adults. Only a tiny minority read the parish bulletin.

For this reason we pay particular attention to providing information for the local correspondent of the *Kilkenny People* and *Carlow Nationalist*. Each group in the parish – including groups that are Church related – are asked to do their own promotion. The following is an example of a press release issued to publicise the pastoral council's programme for the Year of the Family. It appeared substantially as it was provided.

PROGRESSIVE PLANS FOR FAMILY CARE

The New Year has started in the parish with a programme of support for the family.

A survey of the parish was made at the end of 1993 in the house to house visitation by clergy and religious. In one form or another in most households there was a degree of helplessness about the quality of family life.

At its final meeting, the outgoing Parish Council devised a

year-long programme to support family life. There will be two high points of this year of concern for the family: A Family Festival during Lent and an ecumenical Mission in the autumn. The UN and the Catholic Church have declared 1994 'International Year of the Family'. Already BBC television has a series of excellent programmes on the state of the family in western societies. Parishioners are being encouraged to video these programmes for future discussion at house meetings throughout the parish in the old station areas.

The programme for the year was launched on the feast of the Holy Family. 'We plan to have a much more progressive response to this year of universal concern for the family than the national contribution of a divisive debate on divorce,' claimed the parish priest referring approvingly to Fr Colm Kilcoyne's article in the *Sunday Press* (2 January 1994).

PARISH COUNCIL

The incoming Pastoral Council will be an elected body. It will have a young person, a man and a woman representing each traditional station area in the parish. It will be the policy-making body dealing with the pastoral needs of the parish. Its first task will be to develop the projects initiated by the outgoing council, providing a desirable continuity. The main programme for this year will touch on support for family life in all its forms.

FAITH DEVELOPMENT

The involvement by the Liturgy group of parish organisations in the weekend masses set the main theme of the year – concern for family. The feast of the Baptism of our Lord was celebrated by making the connection between baptism and the groups in the parish that support family life. The faith itself was high-lighted as its principal support. Christian values make love a commitment that preserves care and fidelity. During the year the faith friends (for confirmation children) and the faith development (post-primary) programmes will be given special emphasis. House meetings during Lent will be attentive to the faith questions of the families in each station area. A special appeal has gone out to parents 'who up to now have rejected the sacramental programme of preparation to think again about their attitude to these helpful aids for parents'. A programme of preparation of parents with children for baptism will now be done on a home basis – with a public celebration of baptism an essential aspect of receiving the sacrament. Even in cases where baptism is administered in emergency the follow-up ceremony of reception into the Church will also be public. There will be special times for public baptisms such as the feast of the Baptism of our Lord, St Patrick's Day, Easter, Pentecost, etc.

PARENTING

As the children return to school the Parents' Council in both schools are being asked to assist organisers in canvassing mem-bers for the Parenting Course. This course meets a parental need to feel that they are not alone in coping with the special disciplinary problems of modern society. The BBC TV pro-grammes reveal that English society has now become aware of the urgent need for such programmes. The parish objective for 1994 is that every parent, male or female will have the bene-fit of this valuable eight-week voyage of discovery. Openness, assertiveness, supportiveness and new parenting skills have been the outcome of the previous course. It has been a first step for many parents to involvement in parish life. Particular emphasis will be placed on the programme for parents of post-primary children. Helping families where the culture of the family is anti-social and where the victims are the children – often subjected to harassment of a verbal, emotional, sexual kind – is a concern.

SOCIAL CONCERN

Helping the family to cope with the social environment that is hostile to its well-being has been a major concern of the outgoing Pastoral Council. A Colliery Christians 'Peace and Justice' Group will meet for the first time on Tuesday 18 January in the meeting room of the Holy Family Convent, Moneenroe. It will strive to apply the social teaching of the Churches to the concrete reality of people's lives in the parish. Initially it will be looking at areas where the ordinary family is the victim of state, financial and legal policies. It will be proposing remedies more in keeping with the Christian vision of life. The other two Colliery Christians groups, Housing and Action for Employment, will intensify their ecumenical work to focus public concern on the basic needs of the family and its members – its primary need for employment and a home, if there is to be human dignity and development.

ELECTION

The nomination papers for the Pastoral Council election will be going out in two weeks. The priests have expressed their gratitude for the outstanding work of the outgoing council. Their successes include the Parenting course, the parish mission development courses as well as establishing Parents' Councils and three Colliery Christian groups (above) and the ongoing work of social and ecumencial unity in the parish.

The parenting programme referred to in our press release above is one of a number: basic parenting programme, teen parenting programme (8+6 weeks); parenting and sex programme (5 weeks); parents assertiveness programme (7 weeks); young adult programme (8 weeks). These are all provided by the Family Caring Trust, 44 Rathfriland Road, Newry, Co. Down, BT34 1LD. Terry and Michael Quinn provide a handbook, leaders' guides, tapes, posters, videos, and also organise training days for Churches, social services and various organisations throughout Ireland and England. This is a non-profit caring trust set up 'for the building up and support of family life'. All its programmes are based on respectful communication and effective discipline in the home.

We also use a local magazine *Deenside* to write messages which are printed exactly as we write them. These messages are of the faith variety – the sort of message that local newspapers would not use. The following is an example from Christmas of 1992:

Christmas is called the season of goodwill: 'God so loved the world that he gave his only Son that we all may have Life through Him. Little wonder then that Christmas is a celebration of love.

Yet for many people there is a terrible feeling of emptiness, dullness and loneliness at Christmas. Where the sparkle and excitement is gone out of life, Christmas too loses its spark. It is said to be 'quiet', 'boring', or even 'sad'. When our feelings don't really matter in a personal way anymore, when lives cease to touch at a personal level, then it is 'not like Christmas anymore'. Where true love decays, the heart is gone out of Christmas, conversation no longer communicates.

People are very good. The goodwill is nearly

always present. We don't really mean to hurt, discourage or stunt another's growth. Who wants to nag, scold, reject or lecture, boss or make others feel used or ashamed. All these ways of criticising damage people. They discourage. They undermine self-confidence and self-respect. They really nibble away at our love for each other.

Emphasising the negative never helps people to change and grow, to trust and care, to sparkle and give love. How different it is when a person makes time for us, listening with understanding? We know that their encouragement of us comes more from the way they think than what they say.

People who work at having a positive frame of mind, who choose to be Christians, who decide to love, nurture our human and Christian growth. This is the spirit of Christmas.

True Christmas love is not just syrupy or sentiment. It is not cards and 'gifts'. It is more than intense emotion. It is a decision to love. 'He humbled himself to become like us in all things, but sin. He did not come to be served but to serve and to give his life ...' Cards and gifts are meaningless unless they express our decision to look for the good and to work at being understanding. They must reflect our appreciation of the other's efforts, strivings, risks and little improvements.

There are times when in our personal relationships, in family and in Church the spirit of Christmas is absent. Many of us have experienced hurt and discouragement where love and understanding was expected. *Somehow it is easier t*o come to terms with the hurt and discouragement in personal and family life. We find it more difficult to do this when it is the Church that hurts us. If our experience of Church is sometimes harshness, rejection, and diminution, the wounds can be deep.

Christmas is a time for healing. It is a time to seek and to give forgiveness. This is how we are taught to make Christmas a celebration of the Prince of Peace and Lord of Love. Those of us who are identified with the Church, in a particular way, need to know when we have failed to show his Love. If love and understanding have been absent make it known to us, show us and help us to love so that the word made flesh can dwell amongst us.

Our prayer for each one this Christmas is that we will have the courage to help and heal each other in the power of the love revealed in the stable at Bethlehem. Go beyond the tinsel and hype and be prepared to take the necessary action.

* * *

From time to time we print our own messages. We had a major assembly in the parish. Three hundred people attended. The pastoral council and the parish clergy sent out a written response to the issues raised to each household. The following is the clergy's message:

Thanks to our young people for their call for a new way. They set a very high standard of involvement for us all by their attendance and honesty at our Youth Assembly on 25 September 1992. They readily admit that the adult community responded both maturely and magnificently at their Assembly on 28 September 1992. As your officially designated leaders, we priests feel that justice demands an official response to the assembly event from us.

OUR RESPONSE

1) Gratitude (including apologies): three hundred people were involved in the exercise – a fantastic turn out.
2) Encouragement: We realise again that given good leadership people respond. We are fortunate to have such committed people in so many parish/community groups giving that leadership.
3) Challenge: The expectations created by such an event are very high, especially in young people. Results are expected. Having been motivated to journey the new way of caring, good intentions need to be turned into concrete action. The success of our team effort depends on each person's personal commitment to action.

OUR ACTION PLAN

The most effective way to get something moving is to have an organised plan. Growth often comes from the surprises of life – welcome or unwelcome. The various parts of our body are united by the heart and directed by the head. As a people we need similar means of channelling our different ways of feeling, thinking, loving, living. To bring this about we plan the following:

a) After each daily mass, the priest will be available in the Church counselling room for one hour. People will be welcome for spiritual/social reasons or to seek clarification, make suggestions or volunteer for a parish service.
b) Differing ways of providing information will be a priority. A bulletin, such as this one will be produced when necessary. Your use of the local notes in the paper will be reviewed. Our notice board contains an account of parish services; those responsible, who the contact person is and the conditions of obtaining them, such as how they are costed

and paid for and our responsibilities within the laws of State/Church.

c) Formation programmes will receive new urgency. The Church is not a democracy. It is our mission to make known the Good News. It invites us to celebration. It calls us to service. Our involvement has to be informed and free. Everyone's voice will be heard.

PARTICULAR ISSUES

The biggest issue as we see it seems to be that of barriers to communication, e.g., between the youth and adult; between need and services already available to serve that need; between what is said and what is heard. Points A and C are an attempt to bridge these communication gaps. Our Easter message also looks at the youth/adult question in its social context. Direct contact with the hall committee ought to sort out any questions about the hall availability – bearing in mind that the hall is not a roof over a street corner but a facility demanding the exercise of responsibility and care, involving financial commitment and legal liability.

UNEMPLOYMENT

Information on NEKDA can be found on page 39 of *The Colliery Christians*. Unemployment, Emigration, and ideas for coping are on pages 2, 3, 4, 5, 10. The place of organisations is in our 'Tree of Life' and can be seen in the centre pages.

DAY CARE

Castlecomer Day-Care Centre serves the people of Clogh Parish. Our contact person with the centre, will provide information re transport (which is available free) to any persons wishing to avail of the many facilities provided at the centre including physiotherapy. Apart from outings, Christmas parties and visitation, a service in the pipeline is the provision of homes for the elderly. This is being pioneered by The Colliery Christians Voluntary Housing Association in conjunction with Ossory Diocesan Voluntary Housing Group.

20 OCTOBER 1992

Tuesday 20 October 1992 is our launch of a New Way. For this we need the help of everyone especially parents.

a) Parents of children in the fifth and sixth classes who wish to have their children confirmed will come to Moneenroe Hall at 9 p.m. to register them for confirmation. When the confirmation is in Clogh the meetings will be in Moneenroe and vice versa. There Martin Kennedy will tell us about the Faith Friends programme and also what part parents will be asked to play in the programme. He will meet the young adults helping to run the programme at 8 p.m. He will also meet with the parish leadership team at 6.30 p.m. to share his insights as a full time lay person in Church ministry.

b) Parents of children from first and second year at secondary school are asked to volunteer for a meeting in Seville Lodge, Kilkenny. The Growing in Faith Together programme will be launched in our diocese. This programme lasts five weeks and is meant to help the confirmed to live out their confirmation in daily living in the face of so much that is evil in our society especially where self will, pushing out God's will, leads to injustice, dishonesty, violence, social breakdown, addiction, the neglect of children and other evils.

c) It is also a day for new attitudes and a change of heart. Some parishioners found it hard to accept the young people's pain at adults attitudes and youth's sense of feeling condemned. At the 'Mayor's Party' on Saturday last those who over-heard the bitterness of some people's comments on us priests and other people who put a lot of energy into trying to build up the parish realised what the youth meant by 'two-faced', 'double standards' and the rest. The tragedy is that the people who engage in this kind of character assass-ination fail to realise that what they do is malicious, grievously sinful and terribly destructive of the energy being exerted in trying to build a caring Christian community.

d) In our New Way we try to serve and encourage the people who knock those who do their best to change their ways. Difference is part of life. Policy disagreement is healthy. Setting standards and honestly looking at how we measure up are good when done justly and constructively. But to question others' motives or to accuse in a personal and offensive way is a destroying cancer in any community. It brings a burden into service that is unnecessary. Since it is adults who must avoid scandal and give good example the youth have given us a real challenge. If our response lacks the care of father and mother it probably lacks the care of Christ.

e) Fundamental to our ongoing formation is adult example in prayer. In the area of praying at home or showing how involvement in the liturgy develops and expresses a true sense of Christian community and fosters our human and spiritual growth, parental leadership is crucial. Christian renewal of parish life is possible only if one is part of the Sunday liturgy and allows it to influence daily action. Only thus can the Church be present and fruitful in parish life and the message of Christ be discovered anew by each generation.

***

The organisations also were involved in evaluating the parish assemblies. They were encouraged to look at the issues arising in their particular area of interest. Our invitation to each parish group was as follows:

Parish organisations will meet on Wednesday 11-11-'92 at 8 p.m. in Moneenroe Hall. Representatives of each group will assemble for the following reasons:
1) To share with each other a brief account of their aims, what they do, where they meet, the number and age range involved.
2) To compare the totality of service with the expectations from the two assemblies and from the meeting of parishioners on 4-11-'92. (This meeting is for people who are not involved in parish groups but whose contribution to building up the Church is through their family life, their work, their care of family, neighbours, relationships. They, together with people who may feel themselves outside the care of the Church will have had an opportunity to put their views forward at the meeting.)
3) To help the Parish Council identify where there is serious need and where there is no means at present of meeting the need.
4) To discover:
   a) The kind of support and help each group needs.
   b) The range of services already in existence, how to contact them and how to volunteer for membership or to participate in them.
The Parish Council wishes to hear from any group that will not be represented so that a report can be presented on their behalf.

***

The most important thing is to involve people in planning some action that should be a consequence of the message. When sending our message to the emigrants we felt it necessary to give them some hope. We felt that platitudes were not enough; returned emigrants stressed this point. Our message said:

> In a parish of very high migration, we continue to regard our emigrants as parishioners in exile, mostly desiring to return. In fact some people who emigrated in the 1930s were interred here in this parish in the 1990s.
>
> We priests live our lives 'away from home'. For some of our classmates this has a more painful and significant meaning. They are in exile in Sydney, Santiago, Singapore or Sacramento. But wherever we live we have chosen to 'go where we are sent'. That is the origin of mission.
>
> Since coming here in 1989, we have made sure that our exiles, emigrants – those who have left voluntarily and those who have been forced to go – are constantly in our prayers and thoughts.
>
> Between us we have visited you on three continents. We wrote to you for St Patrick's Day 1991 to involve you in our parish mission which opened on that weekend. As we remembered you on Emigrant Sunday, your families at home financially supported the Church's Emigrant Welfare services. At Christmas 1991 your names were the ones on the Christmas tree in our Church. We brought you home in our hearts for the mass, celebrating the joyful news of 'peace on earth'.
>
> This parish magazine was prepared especially with you in mind. Inside you will read of our work as Churches to mobilise the community to strive to overcome a scandal which forces people to leave home against their will. It is in that spirit of concern for you that Dr Robert McCarthy joins us in greeting you and praying for you on this St Patrick's Day.
>
> As you feel new stirrings of pride in faith and fatherland, we want you to know that our love for you

at home, moves us, not to 'drown the shamrock', but to make space for your return, should you so desire.

Meanwhile may you enjoy this festival of our world-celebrated ancestor in the faith, drawing love and hope from his rich inheritance.

The above message was put by the families of emigrants at home into The Colliery Christians, a booklet prepared by the Parish Pastoral Council and sent to emigrants to arrive in time for St Patrick's Day.

The response was so positive that we are now certain that our emigrants should be borne in mind in all aspects of our pastoral planning.

APPENDIX 6

Often we give wrong answers because we have been asked the wrong questions. The set of question given here may not be the correct ones to produce a comprehensive pastoral plan in every circumstance. However, they may be helpful to some parish organisations and pastoral groups in devising more appropriate ones for them.

The seven points below are the summaries of the issues raised in the seven chapters of this book.

1　Note changes in people, in society and in the way we relate to and support one another. How does this help us grow in understanding?

2　In a more open world: the way to discovery, new styles of leadership, bringing new structures to parish – all demand new forms of service in a more independent society. What are the implications for priest and people?

3　What makes leadership credible? What makes the Christian community credible? What does this ask for in the way we relate? What effect does this have on the Church? How does it open the way to the Spirit?

4　Changing our image of God. Why is it necessary? How was/is it achieved? What does it do for prayer, for our liturgy, for our life, for personal renewal, for the renewal of the Church?

5　How does life itself effect us? The influence of our culture and traditions, the gifts that we receive from God, their effect upon the community, the community's effect upon them – how can we draw them into a single community?

6　What are the difficulties? The problems in searching for

services, in struggling for justice, in healing the broken, in strengthening the family, in putting love in the heart.

7 How does the human affect the pastoral? How does the divine touch the real? How does the priesthood interact with ministry? How is pastoral planning creative and respectful of the person?

The following questions refer to the five sections of each chapter. Each should be read.

Chapter 1

1 In your life story tell of a special moment when you were deeply touched by an experience of unconditional love. Recall when faith, hope and love gave someone's personal story a profoundly different meaning.

2 Are you aware of having changed? What stages did your religious and moral growth go through which affected the way you looked at other people and at society's institutions?

3 How does the growth in your life help you have a new vision of the Church? What characteristics of the modern Church 'speak' to your own experience, bringing you to a 'new level and language of faith'?

4 What helps you cope with your own struggles and vulnerability in a world of 'evolutionary change'? What helps overcome fear of rejection?

5 Where, how and with whom do we develop a Christian vision of the world and our relationship with the environment, other people and God?

Chapter 2

1 Do you agree with the Irish bishops that a Church of community and participation is the way of faith? And that belonging, service, scripture and silence are four rich elements of our Catholic tradition? Mention examples of how each has helped you personally.

2 How do people who share a common vision of the Church

experience a sense of vibrant belonging and sharing, as it brings about a vital Christian community?

3 In the growth and development of your parish, how can people's participation become more effective in identifying its area of need and how can they integrate the faith in their response?

4 What are the essential differences in working with rather than for people?

What is the difference between the authoritarian and collaborative style of leadership? Can an authority relationship be totally neutral? How, when, where?

5 How can self-expression, participation, a sense of confidence and self-worth become as important to community development as they are in overcoming personal isolation and alienation?

Chapter 3

1 How do we earn the right to be heard and heeded so that leadership may have authoritativeness and credibility?

2 If we make the creation of community and right relationships within the focus of our attention and energy, how do we strengthen the unity we have in the body of Christ?

3 When authoritarianism, clericalism and legalism have lost their value as ways of creating union, involvement, and accountability in the Church are there alternatives?

4 How is it possible to replicate in the Church the way authority is exercised in the family and in the wider society?

5 When the Spirit leads our personal and parish life what are the fruits which give testimony of his presence in community life?

Chapter 4

1 What helps us to discover where God is present in our lives? How can we make ourselves open to renewal in his image?

2 How do we show that we are social beings in the human and the spiritual senses and animate our community with

the presence of Christ?

3   Give an account of an event in which you have seen life celebrated in liturgy and felt it bring a new dimension to your life.

4   Is it possible to have diversity and the freedom to disagree without threat of oppression? Can our pastoral policy tolerate individuality and a variety of perspectives?

5   What are the benefits for the Church when such 'youthful' characteristics as a spirit of adventure, curiosity about life, hunger for new experience and a passion for freedom are given an honoured place?

Chapter 5

1   Are there issues in your culture and tradition that impinge on how people see God, religion and even life itself?

2   What are the obstacles to our trusting people to have sufficient discernment that they may be given more than just token involvement in parish decision-making?

3   Suggest structures that will help the living entity, the parish, discover common ideals, promote Christian values, accept new ideas and manage change that is rooted in the ethos of each member of the community?

4   Suggest ways that parents, as the prime educators of their children, can be moved from consultation to participation and be persuaded that the school is a main source of Christian ethos.

5   Can parents be supported in their role in a culture which has elements inimical to the well-being of their children?

Chapter 6

1   List some reasons why young people feel especially alienated from Church and state institutions. Have we any means of confronting the causes of this alienation?

2   How can a parish pastoral programme relieve the apathy or anger into which the alienated feel they have been driven? Can the social teaching of the Church help restore

them in dignity?

3 Has the Church a response to the break-up of traditional culture, moral disintegration in society and worldwide spiritual hunger?

4 How do we use the identified gifts of baptised Christians so that there is a unified mission to the poor and hurt and realise the ideal of a missionary Church of Christ?

5 How can the open Christian family (long been regarded as the best model of Church) be utilised to reveal Christ's care and help us to his ideal of self-giving love?

Chapter 7

As sharers in the mission of the word,

1 What do we contribute as persons?

2 When and where are we called to be prophets of love?

3 How do we share in Christ's priesthood?

4 How does this involve us in pastoral collaboration?

In moving towards a collaborative style of ministry the priest shares with the laity and religious in these exercises. They should share the priest's evaluation of himself. The following thoughts are provided to help make this evaluation. Such exercises have proved very affirmative and morale-boosting.

THE PRIEST EVALUATES HIMSELF

In a time of low morale priests need encouragement to admit the existence of strengths as well as weaknesses. The daily 'particular examine' has a sin and sorrow focus. Seeing signs of grace in our talents, skill and commitment reassures us and makes us more effective ministers. Such confidence is not a call to pride but to thanksgiving and wonder at God's bounty. It fulfils our legitimate need for recognition and appreciation. We are enabled to work more efficiently and collaboratively. Proper examination of conscience implies accountability to ourselves, our clients and God.

We might look at the matter this way:

1 We start with our most frequent emotional state: inhibition, anger, depression, ease, cheerfulness ...? What are the negative aspects? Low self-esteem, loneliness, fear, too great expectations ...?

2 What credits may we claim? Fidelity to prayer, dignified and sensitive liturgies, effective involvement of others in ministry, compassionate outreach to those in every kind of pain? What strengths have we in leadership, relationships, administration, counselling, spiritual direction, securing the laity's position?

3 What help is there 'out there' to lighten our burdens?
(Those who have given support to the Clogh clergy include:
   a) Group leaders in our Tree of Life, especially teachers, Holy Family sisters and parish team members
   b) Personnel from Ossory: pastoral group, CMAS, charismatic and youth services, bereavement support, catechetical centre, Focolare and girl guides
   c) Diocesan services such as the liturgy, Lourdes pilgrimage and housing for the elderly committees, marriage preparation courses, CPSMA, CURA, the vocations team and the Peace in Christ retreat house. Also much help from neighbouring clergy and parishes.)

4 It is important also in the light of current priorities to list the initiatives of lay involvement and in advancing the role of women in the Church that we priests take, for example:
   – in areas of service to dependency and poverty
   – in sharing leadership and mission
   – in helping the laity in their role of bringing Christianity into the secular domain: family life, education, health care, employment ...
   – in creating a vibrancy in worship and enthusiasm for biblical and liturgical prayer
   – in utilising the rediscovery of meditation, indigenous forms of prayer, spiritual conselling, prayer and

   scripture study groups
- in assisting people, so traumatised by conflict, between
  their personal experience and accepted views, that their
  world of meaning collapses
- in forming a vital community life using a collaborative
  model of parish with forthright leadership in an ecumenical and civic service
- in devising methods of communicating the message as
  teacher and animator of teachers while being also aware
  of unwelcome parts
- in providing parallel methods and opportunities for
  knowledge of self, roles and relationships, of the local
  environment and its norms, roots and rules
- in maintaining ongoing reflection in the midst of rapid
  change in modern culture.

5 We need to allocate appropriate time to our different roles,
   as builder of community, leader of worship, proclaimer of
   the word, administrator, prophet of dignity and justice,
   minister of reconciliation and consoler of the hurt. We need
   to be aware of our motivation and find a balance between
   personality, conviction and skill. Nor may we forget our
   significance as a religious symbol as one who calls, gives
   example and encourages fellow Christians to share their
   riches, in every sense.

6 Here is a checklist against which we may evaluate our
   effectiveness: dependability, realistic objectives, good
   follow-through, co-operative attitudes, listening ability,
   making space for others, accepting and implementing the
   view offered by parish advisory groups, personal participation in parish training programmes, facing the challenge
   of change.

7 Our vocation and ministry is God's gift; we are called to
   build the kingdom of God amid the people. We are only a
   tiny part of the Church's ministry, though Matthew 25 is a
   salutory reminder about the use of talents. We must continue to furbish these skills.

We are accountable to ourselves, to those we are sent to serve and to the God who sends us for personal growth and self-development. Our people are instinctively aware of this accountability.

Evaluation, clearly a crucial part of our ministry, is probably important for the effectiveness of pastoral planning. Does this not require a shift from a condition of 'fear of letters written with the crozier' to full acceptance of our responsibility?

An evaluation process which shows a positive concern for individual dignity, freedom and responsibilty would help us all to become truly human and necessary ministers of the gospel.

8   What do you think? With whom would you like to share your thoughts? When? Where? How? Why?

APPENDIX 7

In order to involve people in the life of the parish and express that life in liturgy so as to make the Church a felt community of participation and dialogue we take the following steps:

1   We try to adjust the mind-set:
> from talking about – to getting done
> from theories about – to discovering actual effects
> from generalities – to specifics

2   We look at people
> to survey the needs (See Appendix 3)
> to consider their environment – cultural, economic, religious
> to determine their areas of interest – children, school, employment, justice, employment
> to seek existing channels, groups, individuals and structures for response, in, for example, parents councils

3   We work *with* rather than *against*, accepting difference with co-operation.
> We strive to be faithful to our own commitment, doing what we have agreed to do.
> We deny built-in permission for obstruction, indifference or egotism in leaders.
> We face the implications personal and of groups willing to be responsible.
> We look at cause and effect identifying linkages or their absence. For example: 'The reason for … is … that they don't teach religion in school any more.'

4   We develop the notion of pilgrimage, a journey in the real known world

a journey of growth, learning, falling back and needing help

a journey that is made both individually and as members of groups

a journey that needs mechanisms, voluntary but needing commitment from group members

a journey as a parish in need of structures (to share leadership within the principles of Church law and to share partnership in discovering pilgrim needs.

5 We try to develop people's awareness to determine their own capacity as individuals and as the people of God.

6 The parish team monitors progress in the parish pilgrim journey, mindful that everyone be given the chance to belong, encouraging involvement, allowing for the taking up of new responsibilities and the shedding of others. (No one, including the PP, needs to know every detail. He lets each group 'get on with it' in the context of overall vision!)

7 Sensitivity to tension points is balanced against over-all need. For example the domination by one person or a small group is rather different from the chairman's duty to ask people to account for the 'solo run' or apathy. Some need to be drawn in: 'I haven't heard what Mary has to say...' or 'Let's have the input of the parents council.' Others need to be helped to accept the feedback as to the effect of their behaviour as group members or individuals on such important elements as morale.

We

− note each other's different perceptions on the outcome of some pastoral action

− watch for the concealed solution when we hear someone say, 'What you need to do is ... ' before the problem's nature is even agreed upon

− remember the who, what, where, when, how or why of each event or plan

− attempt to identify the main issues for which there is consensus

− seek suggestions for practical action and deal with such

questions as; 'Is this for us?' 'Have or can we get the authority?' 'Have we the facts?' 'Do we really want to...?'

8   We look at the *why* as well as the *who*, at the *how* as well as the *where*.

Examples:

Why does unquestioning acceptance leave people in a groove?

What seems perfectly obvious to you that is far from obvious to someone else?

When does uniformity of thinking and action limit growth?

How does one learn to take into account other points of view, identifying fences that restrict thinking?

How does your past experience, expectations, concerns, your idea of God and what his Church teaches influence your attitudes and responses?

9   We consider situations and our response to them: we say to people:

Notice the way in which you look at that part of an issue which has most meaning for you. As you may see in Appendix 1 for the miners the focus was justice and for the bishops communism. This gave two entirely different aspects both valid but less than the whole truth. The more limited view brought entrenchment – victory needs power.

The solution is often not the problem – a new analysis gets a new focus.

10 To maximise creative thinking we identify obstacles. They include:

- instant evaluation: 'That's cracked / foolish / impossible / heretical / disloyal ...'
- playing it safe: 'Don't risk looking foolish.' 'You'll only make trouble.' 'People won't accept it.' 'People expect it to be that way.'
- searching for 'right' answers, 'perfect' ideas, total approval

We also use the following aids: